AN AVERAGE JOE'S PURSUIT FOR FINANCIAL FREEDOM

AN AVERAGE JOE'S PURSUIT FOR FINANCIAL FREEDOM

CHANGE YOUR PERCEPTION OF MONEY

MICHAEL WARREN MUNSEY

Copyright © 2014 by Michael Warren Munsey.

Library of Congress Control Number: 2014903579
ISBN: Hardcover   978-1-4931-7768-4
           Softcover   978-1-4931-7769-1
           eBook   978-1-4931-7767-7

All rights reserved. No part of this book may be reproduced or transmitted in any form or by any means, electronic or mechanical, including photocopying, recording, or by any information storage and retrieval system, without permission in writing from the copyright owner.

This book was printed in the United States of America.

Rev. date: 04/09/2014

To order additional copies of this book, contact:
Xlibris LLC
1-888-795-4274
www.Xlibris.com
Orders@Xlibris.com
551802

TABLE OF CONTENTS

Introduction 9

Chapter 1—What Is Being Financially Free? 13
    Expectations of Being Financially Free 14
    Pensions 16
    401(k) Retirement Plans 17
    Social Security 17

Chapter 2—Education 22
    How Schools Measure Success 23
    Working for a Paycheck 25
    Should We Give Our Finances to a Financial Planner? 25
    Increase Your Financial Intelligence 26
    Get Your Spouse on Board 27
    Negatives of a Formal Education 29
    How Risk-Averse Are You? 30

Chapter 3—What Are Assets and Liabilities? 33
    Stand Out among Investors 33
    The Importance of a Job 35
    Is Your Home an Asset? 35
    Is Gold an Asset? 37

    The Gold Standard 38

    Benefit and Negative of Currency Set to a Gold Standard 39

    Is Cash in a Savings Account an Asset? 40

    Interactive Exercise.. 40

    Calculate Your Net Worth 42

Chapter 4—Getting Control of Spending 43

    Calculate Your Cash Flow 44

    The Cost of Vehicles 46

    Value of Entertaining 50

    Spending on Vacations and Entertainment............................... 51

    Standard of Living 52

Chapter 5—Increasing Your Income 56

    Think Out of the Box to Create Additional Income 59

    Do Not Let Fear Be an Obstacle 61

    Overcoming Self-Doubt and the Naysayers.............................. 63

Chapter 6—Leverage, Good and Bad Debt 64

    Leverage 64

    Bad Debt Equals Liabilities 65

    Good Debt Equals Assets 66

    Excuses for Increasing Bad Debt 68

    Reasons for Not Increasing Good Debt................................... 68

    Balancing the Ratio between Good and Bad Debt..................... 70

    Take Care of Your Credit Score 73

Chapter 7—The Importance of Setting Goals 74
- Elements of a Successful Plan to Meet Your Goals 74
- Know What You Want to Achieve 75
- Set Goals That Are Attainable 77
- Set Goals That Are Measurable 79
- Measurable Aspects of a Goal 80
- Set Short-Term Goals to Meet a Long-Term Goal 80
- Yearly Steps to Reach My Goal 81
- Commitment and Sacrifice to Meet Your Goals 82
- Your Plan Should Be Flexible 83
- Make Yourself Accountable 84
- Celebrate Your Accomplishments 86

Chapter 8—Creating Passive Income 88
- Ways to Generate Passive Income 89
- Persistence in a Long-Term Passive Income Strategy 90
- Choosing an Investment Vehicle to Generate Passive Income 90
- Flipping Houses vs. Rental Property 91
- No One Needs an Additional Job 92
- Outline a Standard to Follow 92

Chapter 9—Building a Team 95
- Mortgage Broker or Banker 95
- Real Estate Agent 96
- Home Inspector 96
- Appraiser 97
- An Insurance Broker or Agent 97

Locksmith 97

Cleaning Crew and Landscaper 98

Home Warranty Policy 98

Property Manager 99

Third Party Walk-Through to Audit Property 99

Accountant and Real Estate Attorney 100

Chapter 10—Recap 101

INTRODUCTION

I am an everyday average Joe searching for a way to become independent from a paycheck and a job. I have to admit that I am not currently financially free, and I am handcuffed to a job in the oil industry. I work for a paycheck to provide for the standard of living I want to provide for my family. One thing you can be assured of is that I practice what I write.

I am ambitious in my aspirations, but I am confident that one day I will be financially free and independent from a paycheck. One day, I will be in a position where my money works for me rather than going to work every day for a paycheck myself. I want to provide a specific standard of living for my family without having to get up and go to work. If you picked up this book looking to learn something new about personal finance, this book is not for you. Every concept in this book has been written or explained by other authors.

I am writing this book for a couple reasons: I want other average Joes trying to get to retirement in the tough world of personal finance to understand that they are not alone. I want to share my personal experiences and struggles on my own finance in an effort to help someone keep from making the same bonehead mistakes that I made when I was in my early twenties and thirties. This book was not written to change your current investment strategy because there is no one set formula in becoming financially free. Each one of us has to find the financial vehicle that works best for us. This book should help you to ask the tough questions about your own personal finance decisions. The journey to be financially free is not easy and should not be taken lightly.

I was raised in a small rural town in Southern Illinois. The primary occupations in the region were coal mining, farming, and oil-field production/services. I graduated from a high school with a class of twenty graduates. My high school had just over one hundred students total. Many of the school districts in the region where I was raised had consolidated multiple surrounding small-town schools with the exception of our small town. Many residences in our town were afraid that if we consolidated with the other school districts and lost our school, our town would lose its identity.

After graduating high school, I went off to college in Murray, Kentucky, at Murray State University. I graduated from Murray State in May of 1995. I got married two weeks after graduation and began working for a civil engineering firm in West Tennessee as a project manager, overseeing construction staking for several highway construction projects in West Tennessee and Northern Mississippi. After working in the civil engineering field for two years, I decided that I would not be able to provide the standard of living that I wanted to provide for my family. My dad put in a good word for me with the company that he was working for at the time, Halliburton Energy Services, which helped me to get my first decent-paying job. The job opening with Halliburton was in Shreveport, Louisiana, so my wife and I packed up and moved to Shreveport, Louisiana, to work in the oil industry. For the next six years, I worked the oil fields in North Louisiana, East Texas, and Mississippi.

After gaining six years of field experience, I interviewed for a promotion in Oklahoma, Dallas, Fort Worth, and Houston. Halliburton decided to send me to Houston, Texas, to work as a desk engineer for a large independent oil and gas operator. At the beginning of 2006, I made a business trip with a colleague to Mission, Texas, to work on a well. Over dinner, we discussed my career and where I wanted to be in the next ten years. We discussed the value in earning my professional engineering license in petroleum versus going back to school to get a graduate degree master of business administration (MBA). My colleague worked to get his professional engineering license and wished that he had gotten his MBA instead.

When I returned from Mission, Texas, I signed up to take my Graduate Management Admission Test (GMAT) and applied to enroll in the Executive Master of Business Administration (EMBA) program at Rice University in Houston, Texas. While earning my MBA, I learned a great deal about business and much more about myself. In the last set of classes just before graduating, I took an entrepreneurship class, which has drastically impacted the direction of my life and decision making. The professor that taught the class consistently talked about making money while you sleep. One way he suggested to make money while sleeping was through the Internet. This sparked my interest, of course, but I am not Internet savvy and I am not very creative. Ironically enough, my wife is in the process of starting up an Internet company.

In the spring of 2009, my employer announced that they were going to restructure the company. For those of you that have not gone through a company restructuring, it is another way of saying "possible layoffs." At that time, I was in the process of reading Robert Kiyosaki's *Rich Dad, Poor Dad*. The problem became very clear while reading this book. I worked for a paycheck rather than having my money work for me. The next question was how long I could live without a paycheck before I went bankrupt. The answer was "not very long." It was the spring of 2009 when I changed my definition of *success*. It took me twelve years into my professional career to decide exactly what my definition of a *successful career* meant to me.

Early in my career, I thought that I wanted to climb the corporate ladder and be a high-paid employee. Now I am striving to be financially free, not working for a paycheck while not lowering my current standard of living. In order for me to be successful, I need to be able to generate enough passive income so I do not have to work for a paycheck to provide for my everyday needs.

CHAPTER 1

What Is Being Financially Free?

Before we get too deep into the subject of personal finance, I think it is best to be clear on the definition of *being financially free*. The definition of *being financially free* may be slightly different from what you have been taught from your parents and in the classroom. The exposure you have to understanding personal finance can also shape your opinion. Over the last several years, our expectations to be financially free and to retire has changed with respect to pensions, saving plans, 401(k)s, Social Security benefits, and a common problem today: our medical coverage during retirement.

When we discuss being financially free in this book, I am referring to having your money work for you. To be truly financially free, you do not need to work for money or have the need to dip into your savings account to live at the standard of living that you have become accustomed to. This includes taking money out of your savings for traveling and vacations. Being financially free is using income that you do not have to work for to pay your daily expenses—housing, food, medical expenses, travel, and entertainment. This income is generated from investments that create passive income rather than depleting the savings you worked so hard to set aside.

Expectations of Being Financially Free

Over the last several decades, the rules of thumb that we use to plan for retirement or being financially free have changed. If you are anything like me, you most likely did not realize that anyone changed the rules for planning for retirement. I did not realize the rules for planning to become financially free had changed until reading Robert Kiyosaki's *Rich Dad, Poor Dad*.

Prior to the Industrial Revolution, the basis of most people's income was agriculture, and the entire economy revolved around agriculture. The Agriculture Revolution began with Neolithic Revolution between twelve thousand to eight thousand years ago. The Neolithic Revolution is the transition from prehistoric hunting and gathering to settlements with an agriculture basis. These settlements with an agricultural basis led to the creation of permanent dwellings with specialized labor, which led to the formation of cities.

The Neolithic Revolution was followed with the Arab Agricultural Revolution between the seventh and thirteenth centuries. Muslim traders began trading different crops and farming techniques across many different parts of the Old World. This trade led to a major shift in the economy, distribution, and agricultural production of citrus fruit and numerous types of crops, which include sugarcane, cotton, and rice. The Arab Revolution interconnected different labors and trades such cooking and clothing, which led to an increase in income and a growth in population.

The Arab Agricultural Revolution led to the British Agricultural Revolution between the seventeenth to the nineteenth century. The British Agricultural Revolution saw an increase of productivity. The increase of agricultural productivity helped to break food shortages and famines that limited the population growth in local territories that did not produce enough goods to sustain the demand of a growing population. The British Agricultural Revolution transformed from a peasant affluence economy to a capitalist agricultural system, which led to more wealth.

In the nineteenth century, we had the Industrial Revolution, which most of us are familiar with. The Industrial Revolution is the transition from handmade manufacturing methods to chemical and machine manufacturing. Improved efficiencies were seen in iron production process and water power, such as steam. The transition from fuels (such as wood) to fossil fuels (such as coal) took place also.

You are probably thinking by now that the history background is nice, but it is not what you are interested in reading about. The Industrial Revolution is a major turning point in history in every aspect of our daily life. Both the population and average income began an extraordinary maintainable growth. Along with the increase in an individual's average income, also came a transition from an agricultural based labor force to a skilled labor force. This transition to skilled labor force also brought into play the thought of retirement.

We are all taught at an early age to go to school, get good grades, work hard, and work for a company (for your entire career) that provides good benefits and a pension. This way of thinking was taught to me as I grew up and is still taught by many parents and in our school systems today. I know I do not have to tell you that times have changed again. We are in a new revolution: the Computer Revolution or Information Age. Since times are constantly changing, so does the way that we plan to be financially free.

I hope you see why I took the time to take you through the historic evolution of progress, all the way back in the beginning of the hunting and gathering age to the Information Age. If you are a historian, you could point out many turning points that could have been used, but all

I was trying to illustrate is that we are in an ever-changing world, and the way we take care of our personal finances must change with the times—or we will be left in the dirt with the dinosaurs.

Pensions

In the Industrial Revolution, it was very common for employees to find a job with a large corporation that offered good retirement benefits and job security. The employees were loyal to the company and typically worked their entire career with one company. In return, the company repaid their loyalty with a pension payment plan upon retirement; the loyalty was mutual between the company and the employee.

A *pension* is a benefit plan that employers provide that guarantees a specific monthly payment or benefit upon the retirement of an employee. This monthly payment is determined by a predetermined formula. The formula consists of the tenure or years of service that the employee served with the employer, the employee's earning history, and the employee's age. Conventionally, many public or governmental benefit packages as well as a large number of large corporations—offer their employees this type of retirement benefit. Pension plans or payments can be passed to the employee's surviving spouse as long as the spouse is properly named as a beneficiary. The pension payments are not typically passed down to additional generations.

401(k) Retirement Plans

In 1978, the 401(k) was created as a result from the Tax Reform Act. The Internal Revenue Code became effective on January 1, 1980. Congress passed the Economic Growth and Tax Relief Act in 2001; this new legislation enabled lower-income workers to afford to contribute into a 401(k) retirement plan with minimum taxation on their contribution. In the middle of the 1990s to early 2000s, corporations and some governmental benefit plans began offering their employees an option to move away from a standard company pension plan to a 401(k) plan. Today, many companies do not offer new employees a pension plan and only offer 401(k) retirement plans.

A 401(k) retirement plan provides the employee more flexibility and control of their retirement funds. The employee can contribute to their 401(k) plan prior to taxes being taken from their paycheck. Also, many corporations will match an employee's contribution, limited to a percentage of an employee's annual salary. The funds in the 401(k) plan can be invested in a number of different investment vehicles such as stocks, bonds, or mutual funds. The 401(k) plans also allow for hardship withdraws at a very high taxation rate. A 401(k) plan can also be passed down to both spousal and nonspousal beneficiaries.

Social Security

Many people that have already retired depend on their Social Security benefits. The majority of the baby boom generation has planned on using their Social Security benefit to supplement their income in their retirement. Social Security was drafted in the first term of Franklin Delano Roosevelt's presidency. The act was designed to address poverty and unemployment by supplementing their income with government assistance. Over the years, the majority of American citizens believe that they are entitled to Social Security benefits simply because so many of us have paid taxes into the Social Security program. It is widely known that the Social Security Trust Fund is in the process of collapsing.

The Social Security shortcoming was realized in the 1980s when the projections of the Social Security Trust Fund fell short of supplying the baby boom generation with their portion of the Social Security benefits. While the baby boom generation is in the workforce and is paying taxes into the fund, we have a surplus in the Social Security Trust Fund. The shortage of funds begins to be a problem when the baby boom generation decides to leave the workforce to retire. The cash flow in the Social Security Program goes from positive to a sharp negative.

In an effort to correct the shortcoming of the Social Security Program, the politicians decided to invest the surplus of the fund. The problem they faced was investing such a large surplus of cash. The surplus was so large, if all the money was invested in the stock market, they would have created a negative effect on the world's markets. The politicians decided to invest in the United States. They used the surplus cash to purchase special bonds from the US Treasury. The problem really came when they decided to take earnings from the bonds and spend the earnings on other interests rather than returning the proceeds to the Social Security Trust Fund. There are many of us that just cannot count on the Social Security program supplementing our income during retirement.

The concern for being financially free escalates when we consider how we are going to pay for our medical costs during retirement. I know that the intent of many of the politicians are good by trying to implement the Affordable Care Act, but this is a problem that will be with us for a long time, which makes planning for retirement or to be financially free that much harder.

We have covered how our economic environment is ever changing, from the evolution of the Agricultural Revolution into the Industrial Revolution, and now into the Computer Revolution or Information Age. The way that we plan to be financially free must evolve as well. Many parents and even the school systems are slow to change their thinking when it comes to planning to be financially free. One reason for the slow change is because the majority of us struggle with our own personal finances. Many of us do not understand how money works. Many people do not take responsibility for their own personal finances. They give the responsibility of their finances to a financial planner. I do not entrust my financial future to a financial planner, and we will cover the concerns with passing on this responsibility in the next chapter.

In school, I was taught to go to school, work hard, get good grades, go to college, and find a job with a good company with benefits. I was also taught that the ones that work hard will succeed. I agree that we should all work hard, but we also have to work smart. There are tremendous amounts of very hardworking Americans that struggle financially and will struggle when it comes to retirement.

A problem with depending on a company's pension plan, a 401(k) retirement plan, and even our Social Security program to supplement our income when we decide to retire is that we are not really financially free. If a pension is a part of your retirement, you are dependent on the guarantee that your former employer will follow through with their promise of supplying you with a predetermined amount of money each month when you reach the retirement age. Are you absolutely 100 percent confident that the formula the company uses to decide how much money you will receive monthly will not change? Even in retirement, you are dependent on your former employer by depending on a pension that you earned but have no control over. You may be able to pass your pension on to your spouse, but what will you leave for your children?

How many people did you know were on the verge of retirement prior to the last recession? How many of them had to postpone their retirement because they had the retirement in a 401(k) account and lost a substantial amount of value in the 401(k) retirement because the stock market took a sharp drop? I live in Houston, Texas, and there are many people in the Greater Houston area that lost their retirement when Enron collapsed. I know that all financial planners will recommend moving the bulk of your retirement savings into *safer,* less-risky stocks that yield lower returns to help ensure that you do not lose a substantial amount of your retirement in poor economic times.

I am no different than the majority of people that choose to read this book; I have a 401(k) saving account also. The difference that I have with my 401(k) plan is that a 401(k) plan is only a savings account. I do not want to have to worry if I have enough money in my 401(k) savings account to live from once I decide to retire. What if you and your spouse are lucky enough to live longer than the life expectancy of your peers? Or will it be a curse because you depleted your retirement too fast and ran out of money in your savings too soon? Will you have to drop your standard of living in order to survive?

Okay, enough of the gloom and doom. I want to be clear about my concerns with company pensions, 401(k) retirement plans, and our Social Security program. These programs are good, but do they make us financially free? I do not think so. This book is not meant to scare you about the choices you have already made; it is meant to make you think about your current investment plan and how you want to move forward.

The million-dollar question is this: how do we invest to become financially free? I do not think that there is one set answer. We all have different needs, wants, and interests; therefore, the amount of passive income that we need to generate to be financially free is different, depending on the standard of living and geographic location we choose to live in. For example, I grew up in a rural part of Southern Illinois and now live in the Greater Houston area. The amount of passive income generated in order to be financially free and live at the similar standard of living should be less if you live in a rural region of the country as opposed to living in a large metropolitan area.

CHAPTER 2

Education

The message that I hope rings loud and clear is that a formal higher education has very little to do with a person's success in business, their career, or even personal finance. That is not to say that education is not important. We should always be striving to learn how to improve ourselves, but we do not need a formal higher education to be successful. There are many outlets for us to learn and educate ourselves without attending a college or university, especially with all the information available on the Internet, in books, and those offered in seminars. The key to be successful at anything is each individual's drive, work ethic, heart, and attitude. I am a firm believer that we can do anything we work at achieving. If you are anything like me, being disciplined enough to be financially free requires a lot of work.

    I do not want to sound like a hypocrite by implying that there is no value in a higher education. My wife and I both went to college, and I want both my boys to get their formal education. On the other hand, there is no doubt that education is not a must. There have been many successful people that did not get a formal education. I am a prime example that you do not have to be smart to obtain a college degree. I am sure that you also know several people that obtained a formal education and are not working in the field that they specialized in while earning their degree.

The ones that have the luxury of obtaining a higher education may have more opportunities available for them than those that did not pursue a higher education. The opportunity itself does not make someone successful; it is the drive and ambition that an individual possesses that will help him or her to take advantage of the opportunity. Additional education also exposes us to many different ideas and opinions from an array of different people that we may not be exposed to once we get in the real world and take on real responsibility and accountability. These are the reasons I want both my boys to pursue additional education.

How Schools Measure Success

Standardized tests, good grades, and even performance in sports are ways we measure our children. Good grades are necessary in order to be accepted into the best schools. Getting into the best schools may open doors that are not available for the average Joe. This can come at a price because our school system teaches our children that less than perfect is a negative characteristic; this negative characteristic is mentally implanted at an early age. We are taught that less than perfect will be graded or viewed less than our friends that get better grades. Majority of the time, there is only one answer to the problem that we are asked to solve. In the real world, it does not necessarily work the same, and many people are afraid of failure. The fear of failure could be a result of how we measure our children in our school system.

If getting good grades comes easy for the individual, they may not learn how to apply themselves. When they face difficult problems out of school, they may not know how to handle being less than perfect. Even though many doctors and lawyers earn a high income, many of them still struggle with finances because they consume too much. Some consume too much simply to maintain a certain *status* in their community, or they do not know how to control their impulses. They may have a very high IQ, but they may not have mastered their emotional intelligence.

Most of us are taught as children that failing a task is a negative aspect in life; therefore, we fear that if we struggle or stub our toe in our pursuit to meeting a goal, others may view us as *failures*. From an early age, we are taught to perform well in school, to perform well in athletics, and to perform well at our *job*. We are pushed not to fail. If we make a mistake or fail, it was and is still today viewed as negative. For this reason, most of us are wary to share our aspirations, expectations, and even goals in life because we do not want to be viewed as a failure if we do not achieve our goals.

Everyone makes mistakes in life; investing is no exception. Anyone that tells you that they have not made a mistake with their investments is not being honest with you, or they simply do not invest. Making mistakes is part of being human and should not be viewed as a failure. Instead, mistakes should be viewed as learning opportunities. Those that do not learn from their mistakes are destined to fail again. We all are going to make mistakes, but learning from our mistakes and not repeating the same mistake twice is the key to reaching our end goal.

Once you set your goal and develop a plan, make sure you tell your friends and your peers that are close to you about your plan and goals. Hopefully, you surround yourself with like-minded individuals that have the similar interests as you have that can help you discuss different strategies. You will be able to learn from one another's experiences, and you might learn something to help you refine your plan to increase the likelihood that you will be able to achieve your goal.

Of course, when you discuss your plan, you will always run across *naysayers*. These types of individuals are afraid to take on risks, and most likely, they do not have experience because they let their fear of failure be an obstacle for investing. Try to surround yourself with individuals with similar goals and aspirations so you can learn from one another's experiences. Make sure you communicate your plan for meeting a goal to make yourself accountable. By making yourself accountable to others, you are more likely to take action on your plan to meet your goal.

Working for a Paycheck

If you are like the majority of us, you have to work for a paycheck. I personally work around sixty hours a week in my profession in the oil-field industry. If I have a deadline, sometimes I may work seventy to eighty hours a week to meet the deadline. This is no different than the vast majority of the American workforce; we do what it takes to get the job done. This is good for us because we are making money for our family, and it is good for our employer, who is making money from our work product.

Should We Give Our Finances to a Financial Planner?

How many people do you know that work extremely hard for a paycheck, doing whatever it takes to get the job done? We work hard for our employer so our employer can make money from our product and pay us well. How many of those same people work just as hard to take care of their own personal business and personal finances? Do they use a financial planner to take care of their personal business or financial affairs for them? If you decide to use a financial planner to manage your investments, I hope you choose a better-than-average financial planner. Hopefully, their investment strategy will grow at the rate they plan. What happens if you pick an average or even a poor financial planner? Will you be able to retire? Do you know enough about investing and finance to identify a better-than-average financial planner, or is your selection based on someone else's opinion?

Increase Your Financial Intelligence

The first step in taking care of your own personal business and finances is not only picking the right investments, but also increasing your knowledge and financial intelligence. It is about managing your finances by educating yourself. Increasing your financial intelligence can range from reading books to taking an individual class or going to a weekend seminar. I am not suggesting that you get a financial degree, but if you need help understanding a specific task or concept, do not be afraid to take a single class from a community college to increase your financial knowledge. My goal when increasing my financial intelligence was to learn how to make my money work for me.

The second portion of increasing your financial intelligence is getting experience by acting on the concepts you learn about. This is the hardest step to take for many investors. It is human nature to feel uneasy when we do something that is outside our area of expertise. It is common for everyone to worry about losing money on their investments. The key is being able to control your emotions and being confident in your knowledge. This is where I am on my journey to financial freedom. I am taking baby steps and not gambling on my investments. The reason I can confidently say I am not gambling is because I have taken the time to increase my financial intelligence. I have also done my due diligence prior to investing any money. Granted my investments are very small investments as compared to many investors, but I am working on increasing my financial intelligence in between investments due to limited money available to invest at one time.

I know from experience that it is not easy to take personal responsibility of your personal finances after a rough and long day at work. For those that want to take the easy way out by hiring a financial planner, you may not want to read this book any longer. For those of you willing to increase your financial intelligence and act on what you have learned, please continue to read and push yourself to be financially free. The road will not be easy. You may lose a little money on investments over time—but learn from your mistakes, educate yourself, and continue to increase your knowledge so you can make your money work for you rather than you working for the money.

Get Your Spouse on Board

Do you know anyone that hates to talk about business or investing? I love my wife, but she can wear you out talking. She had no interest in talking about investing. In the past, she had been known for saying the following:

"You take care of the investing."

"I trust your decisions."

"We did okay on the last investment, whatever you think is best."

My wife loves to talk and talk, but when it came to investing, she had no interest. It has only been a few years since we started investing and I can now talk to my wife about investing without her eyes glazing over with boredom. She was taking the easy way out of investing by depending on my decisions—by not taking an interest in understanding our investment strategy.

A few years ago, I began reading the book *Rich Dad, Poor Dad* by Robert Kiyosaki; and about halfway through the book, I had decided that I needed to change the way I viewed money, my attitude, our spending habits, and our investment strategy. I knew that I needed my wife's help to be successful to make such a major change to our core values and the way we viewed money. The problem I had was that my wife hated the type of books that I liked to read. She typically read novels similar to those by John Grisham and Danielle Steel. I explained some of the key concepts from the book and told her that we were about to make some major changes. I told her that if she wanted to understand the reason I have decided to make such a major change in my thinking and lifestyle, she needed to read *Rich Dad, Poor Dad*. Lucky for me, once she picked up the book, she could not put it down. She actually finished the book before I did.

There are several reasons you need to get your spouse involved with your investment strategy. In order to maximize your investments, you both must be able to control your spending habits. You must be disciplined enough to put aside a predetermined amount of money just for investing each month. It is also very easy to spend your proceeds from your investments once you make a little money, but you both must be disciplined enough to reinvest your profits. Once you put your money in the investment column, do not take it out. You both need to understand your investment strategy. You need to be able to continue to take care of the investments in the event, heaven forbid, that something happens to either one of you. You should not want your spouse to struggle financially if something bad were to happen to you.

Negatives of a Formal Education

I don't have to tell you that a formal education is very expensive. It has been reported that many graduates struggle to pay back their student loans after obtaining their degree. A large number of graduates acquire large debt with student loans and, in some cases, very large credit card debt by choosing to obtain higher education. The question we have to ask is this: what is the value of obtaining a higher education? Is getting a formal education worth the stress and money it takes to obtain a formal degree?

There is no doubt that I have benefited from earning my education, but I am still paying for my school. I graduated high school in 1991 and received my undergraduate degree from Murray State University in 1995. I decided to go to graduate school in the summer of 2005 and graduated to earn an MBA from Rice University in 2007. I have been paying student loans since 1995 and am anticipating making my last student loan payment in 2016. I don't regret making my payments every month on my student loans for a total of twenty-one years because I have a career that I love. I would not have been able to have the career I currently enjoy and give my family the many things I have been able to without getting a formal education. On the flipside, there is a large majority of college graduates that cannot say the same.

How Risk-Averse Are You?

A key to anyone's success is their ambition, drive, and maybe more importantly, how tolerant they are to risk. The reason I threw in the topic of tolerance to risk is because we all have to be willing to step out of our comfort area in order to succeed. The risk could be as simple as moving away from your hometown and leaving a secure job with limited opportunity for a new opportunity with a little uncertainty and unlimited potential. It could also be making the decision of which investment will give the highest return on your investment.

How many people do you know of that will not leave their hometown to search for work? If you have made that choice to move away from your hometown, family, and friends, you understand when I say it is a sacrifice. I made the choice sixteen years ago to move fourteen hours from my hometown, family, and friends to pursue an opportunity to work in the East Texas and North Louisiana oil fields. I chose to move away in an effort to provide a higher standard of living for my family as opposed to the standard of living that I could provide if I lived near the town where I was raised. The major sacrifice for my family is that we are not able to spend as much quality time with my family.

I am lucky that we have been able to maintain a close relationship with my family despite the fact that we only get to spend about a week or two together each year. The ones that are affected the most by the long distance are my boys. They love the time that they spend with their grandparents and aunt, but there is never enough time for them. My oldest has a hard time relaxing. He cannot enjoy the time that he spends with my family because he dreads the day they have to leave and go back home to Texas. It does not matter if he is visiting for four days or four weeks; he always counts down the days that he has before he must leave. Moving away from our hometown, family, and friends is a sacrifice for me and my wife.

Many people are not willing to take a chance in changing jobs. It is hard for many of us to make the choice to leave a comfortable position with a secure job. Stepping out of a comfortable role with an existing job into a job with a little uncertainty is difficult for many people to make. I have made three career changes since graduating college in 1995. The first decision I made to leave a job with a civil engineering firm in Western Tennessee to take my first job in North Louisiana to work for Halliburton was not a difficult decision because I was able to double my income and begin a profession that had unlimited opportunity. The second decision I made to leave Halliburton after working nine years to go to work for a large independent oil company was a little more difficult because I was very comfortable in my current role with a very large company. I took the leap and have not regretted it. The last job change was when I was asked to leave a large independent oil company to go work for a startup oil company backed by a private equity. Each decision to move was a little harder, but I have not regretted any of the decisions I made. If and when you decide to make a major life-changing decision, don't ever second guess your decision and move forward.

When I started this chapter, I wanted to make sure to convey the message that a formal higher education has very little to do with a person's success in business, their career, or even personal finance. Many people throughout history have become financially free without obtaining a formal education. Just a few people that did not finish or seek a formal education that you may know of are Mary Kay Ash, founder of Mary Kay Inc. (the cosmetic company); Richard Branson, owner of the Virgin brand; Simon Cowell, television producer and judge for the television talent show *American Idol*; Michael Dell with

Dell Computers; Walt Disney, creator of Mickey Mouse; Henry Ford, who left home at the age of sixteen to become a machinist; Bill Gates with Microsoft; and Milton Hershey, who started his own chocolate company. Each one of these successful people has a couple of things in common. They decided not to obtain a formal education, they followed their passion, and they were not afraid to step out of their comfort zone. They were willing to take a little risk in order to pursue something big. Anyone that is lucky enough to be truly financially free understands how to make their money work for them, and they also have enough discipline to control their spending.

CHAPTER 3

What Are Assets and Liabilities?

From the last chapter, we discussed how the school systems measure our children. We are told to get good grades and get a good job. We are also taught that our home is an asset, to save for retirement, to find a financial planner, to diversify, and that debt is bad. This advice had always made sense to me because everyone I talked to gave me the same recommendation. We are all taught the same formula for personal finance and investing. It was not until I read *Rich Dad, Poor Dad* that I began to look at investing and personal finance from a completely different perspective. This formula is great if you want to invest like the majority of investors. The question is this: can you become wealthy by investing like the majority? I would say it is possible, but it is more difficult if you follow the pack of the majority.

Stand Out among Investors

One of our many responsibilities as a parent is to teach our children how to be responsible with their money. One problem with teaching our children about managing their personal finances is that personal finance is something that the majority of families struggle with themselves. Most of us learn how to manage our personal finances from our education system and our parents. This problem is evident when there is such a large discrepancy between the top 1 percent of wage earners and the rest of the wage earners. Many in our society are on a mission to make the top 1 percent of wage earners into villains. It is a sad day in America when so many of our citizens embrace this way of thinking. Our founding fathers eventually escaped the tyranny of the government and revolted over taxes imposed by England on the ones that settled in the New World. The only reason I make this distinction between the top 1 percent of wage earners versus the remaining 99 percent of society is simple; they view assets, liabilities, and money much different than the rest of society.

It is easy for the majority of the have-nots to lash out against the top 1 percent of wage earners. It is much harder to look at ourselves in the mirror and admit that we have a spending problem and/or that we do not understand how to manage our own personal finances. How many stories have we heard of about someone winning the lottery and, a couple years later, find himself flat broke? It is not the amount of money someone possesses that enables him to be on the top 1 percent of wage earners. It is the way the top 1 percent views the way to use their money. On the other hand, there are also stories of people that lose their fortune just to turn around and make it back, just as Donald Trump and Dave Ramsey have done. The reason some people can rebound from bad times or bad decisions by repeating successful earnings is because they understand how to manage their personal finances; they view the world differently than the majority. The top 1 percent of wage earners are not born with the ability of knowing how to utilize their money so that they do not have to work for a paycheck like they were taught to. They could have been taught to take the time to educate themselves by a parent or mentor. It is our responsibility to educate ourselves and act on what we learn in order for us to understand how money works.

The Importance of a Job

Everyone needs a good job to gain life experiences, and if you are lucky, you can earn excess cash to invest. The problem with a good job is that you are working for a paycheck, and you are working to make someone else wealthy. What happens if you lose your job? What happens if you get sick and cannot work for a paycheck? Will the money you earn go away with the job? Rather than working for money, we need to find a way to let our money to work for us. I know that is easier said than done.

We should work for experience, not a just a paycheck. This concept is one that I struggle with myself. By working for experience rather than a paycheck, we should be looking for jobs that challenge us and teach us new concepts in business. By always being on the lookout for opportunities that teach us more about business, we should be able to increase our value to an employer, which should equate to a higher paycheck. With the additional experience, you should be able to make better personal finance decisions that will also help you to become free from a paycheck and a job.

Is Your Home an Asset?

Many of us are taught that our home is an asset. We are consistently told on television commercials or hear radio advertisements daily stating that our home is an asset. Typically, these commercials are selling a service or production for homes. These commercials play on our emotional tie to our home. The advertisers want you to think that by purchasing their product or service, you are *investing* in your home, which they claim is an asset. The statement that your home is an asset is true for our mortgage lender and the government, but your home is actually a liability for you. We are not taught that our homes are liabilities.

What happens if we failed to pay our property tax? We will lose the rights to occupy our home or property; therefore, our property is an asset for the government. Our home is also an asset for our mortgage lender because the mortgage company generates excess cash flow each month from the interest that they charge on the mortgage of our home. If you are lucky enough that the value of your home appreciates over the time that you own it, your home will most likely not be considered an asset. The only way your home would be considered an asset is if your home appreciates in value more than the total money you spent to purchase the home, along with the additional money you spent for improvements and the yearly taxes you paid while owning the property.

The simplest way to explain the difference between an asset and a liability is that an asset puts money in your pocket, and a liability takes money out. If your expenses—such as mortgage, property tax, and maintenance—exceed the revenue you generate upon selling your home, then your house is a liability.

Is Gold an Asset?

In any channel that we tune to, television or radio, we hear commercials promoting the purchase of gold as an investment. Granted if you time the market right, gold can be a good investment and an asset; but if you don't, gold can also be a liability. If you purchase gold at the peak of the market and the price of gold falls below the purchase price, then the gold you just bought should be considered a liability until the price of gold exceeds your purchase price.

If an investor bought gold at the peak of the market in 1980, the gold investment would not have been an asset until twenty-seven years later in September of 2007 when the price of gold finally exceeded the purchase price that you bought your gold for in 1980. Do you want to take the chance in today's market of waiting twenty-seven years to make a profit?

I definitely do not have a crystal ball. I am working hard to become financially free by generating passive income by investing in real estate that provides positive cash flow. Even though I expect to experience inflation in the US dollar with the current state of Washington, DC, politics, I do not feel comfortable investing in gold when I feel that we are close to the peak of the gold market. Just as we saw the price of gold drop in 1980, the price of gold is falling here in 2013 because the economy appears to have hit its bottom, and we are beginning to recover. The perception of either a strong or weak US economy and the strength of the US dollar is a driver for the value of gold, just as it did in 1980 after Ronald Reagan gained the confidence of the American consumer and investors.

Without a doubt, I am sure that the gold market will explode again just as it did in 2007 due to the escalating national debt, which makes the value of the US dollar weak. I am not looking to get rich quick by gambling on the stock market or even the gold market. I want to invest for the long-term, sound investments that provide positive cash flow for the future. The only reason I can see myself investing in gold is to protect my cash from losing value due to inflation.

The Gold Standard

In order to understand how money works, we have to understand the pros and cons of our monetary system on the gold standard. A gold standard is a monetary system that references the value of currency to a specific weight and purity of gold. In the 1780s, the United States adopted the silver standard. In April 1792, Congress passed the Mint Act, which established the United States Mint to produce and circulate currency or coinage in the form of silver dollars. The discovery of gold in 1848 both in California and Australia increased the supply of gold, which caused the price of gold to fall comparative to the price of silver, which led to the Independent Treasury Act of 1848. The Treasury Act of 1848 placed the US currency on a firm currency standard.

In 1971, President Richard Nixon pushed to end the gold standard set in 1848. In 1973, the United States ended the conversion of the US dollar to gold. If you regularly listen to any financial show, you will hear someone making the statement that we should have never taken our currency off the gold standard. I tend to agree that we should have never strayed away from honoring the gold standard for the US currency. The way I understand it, the reason for taking our currency off the gold standard was due to the uncertainty that came about with the additional expenditure acquired during the Vietnam War. The United States lost its global economic influence beginning when France reduced its dollar reserves by exchanging them with gold. The

US currency had repetitively devalued between 1971 and 1973 with respects to the weight and purity of gold, which strongly influenced the government officials to take the US currency off the gold standard.

Benefit and Negative of Currency Set to a Gold Standard

For every benefit we identify for standardizing our currency to the weight and purity of gold, we can also identify a negative. When a gold standard is imposed on currency, significant inflation to the currency is limited because the supply or value of money is directly proportional to rate as the gold reserves increase. I was to the understanding that low inflation was a good aspect of setting currency to a gold standard but not if it restricts the rate that the economy can grow. As an economy's productivity increases, the supply of money has to increase proportionally to maintain sustainable growth. The additional capital is needed to feed the needs of a growing economy. If the growth of the economy exceeds the supply, the economy will starve and regress. The amount of gold deposits or mines could either be an unfair advantage for the countries that are lucky enough to have additional gold deposits as a resource or a disadvantage for those countries that do not have gold deposits as a resource to mine. The answer to the question for a country to set its currency to a gold standard is very complex; therefore, you can see why experts have differing opinions.

Is Cash in a Savings Account an Asset?

Saving money is always better than consuming material possessions, but is cash in a savings account an asset? The problem with saving money in a savings account is that it is possible that you may lose value of your money every day that it sits in your account. If inflation is higher than the interest that you earn by putting your money in a savings account, you lose the purchasing power or value of your money. We are taught to save money from our parents and from our education system. Most likely, it is because that is what their parents taught them. Many people like the security that comes with their excess cash sitting safe in a savings account. Many people think like this, and this is one difference between the 99 percent and the top 1 percent of wage earners. The top 1 percent know how to make their money work for them rather than settle with collecting the minimum interest rate that comes with the typical savings account. It is not that difficult to characterize the difference between an asset and a liability. Are we taught the correct definition? We have discussed that your home is actually a liability.

Interactive Exercise

In order to help illustrate why your home is a liability, let's take a minute and estimate the dollar amount for the questions below. Take the time to grab a pencil and write down the answer to the questions below.

- What price did you pay to purchase your home?
- How much interest do you pay for your home loan?
- What is the yearly cost to insure your home?

- How much do you spend a year on property tax?
- How much do you spend on maintenance yearly?
  —Lawn care
  —Air filters
  —Cleaning supplies
  —Paint
  —Repairs
- Multiply your yearly cost by the number of years you plan to live in your home.
- Total the purchase price of your home, the interest from your home loan, and the multiplied yearly cost to maintain your home.
- What is the market price of your home minus closing costs?

Does the market price of your home minus closing costs exceed the purchase price and yearly expenses of your home? If it does not, your home is a liability. If it does, you are one of the very few people that can claim your home as an asset. For most of us, our home is an asset for the bank that owns your mortgage and the government that collects your property tax. If it is not possible to create positive cash flow from owning your property, it will always be a liability.

The way I define an asset is simple. When you sell your *asset*, did the cash you put in your bank exceed the original purchase price plus expenses used to own the *asset*? If you put additional cash in the bank, then I would define your possession as an asset; if not, it should be a liability. Vehicles, boats, motorcycles, swimming pools, and computers are all examples of liabilities.

Most of us have invested in the stock market. If the price you sell your stock plus dividends exceeds the purchase price of your stock, then you have an asset, but if you have ever lost money on a stock, then it would be a liability. Today purchasing gold is the rage due to the uncertainty of our economy. The next time you purchase anything, ask yourself whether or not this item is an asset or a liability.

Calculate Your Net Worth

It is time for another interactive exercise. Take the time to get a pencil. Write in the book, get a separate piece of paper, or if you want to, build a spreadsheet on the computer. Banks will calculate your net worth to help evaluate your finances. When your finances are on paper, how do your personal finances look? Are you overextended?

Net Worth Calculator			
Personal Assets		Liabilities and Outstanding Debt	
Cash, Money Markets, Savings	$	Mortgage Loan Debt	$
Stock and Bond (Excluding Retirement)	$	Car Loan(s)	$
Estimated Home Value	$	Student Loan(s)	$
Other Real Estate	$	Credit Card Debt	$
Blue Book Value of Automobile(s)	$	Other Debt	$
Other Assets	$		
Total Assets	$	Total Liabilities	$
Total Asset—Total Liabilities			

CHAPTER 4

Getting Control of Spending

When you hear Wi-Fi, Bluetooth, 4G, high-speed, high definition, 1080p, Blu-ray, LCD, smartphone, and iPad, what comes to your mind? First thing that comes to my mind is high-priced toys. These gadgets are a weakness of mine, but my wife could take them or leave them. I tend to spend money where she would rather do without to save money. Have you ever bought something, thrown a party, or taken a vacation with the justification that you deserve it? There is nothing wrong with rewarding yourself or loved ones by splurging on material items or going on a nice vacation, but it should not take precedence over being fiscally responsible. It is important to celebrate our accomplishments by rewarding ourselves for reaching certain financial goals set from a previous year.

Controlling spending is difficult for most of us to do. After reading the book *The Millionaire Next Door* by Thomas J. Stanley and William D. Danko, I decided to work on my spending habits. Believe me, some days are better than others when it comes to being disciplined about spending money. *The Millionaire Next Door* suggests that the majority of first-generation millionaires do not live flamboyantly. They do not drive expensive luxury vehicles. They do not own extravagant homes and do not wear Rolex watches. Just because someone drives around in an expensive luxury vehicle, wears Rolex watches, or live in an extravagant home does not mean that he is rich or even wealthy. He may have acquired a large amount of debt and may be living above his means in order to purchase nice material items.

My wife recently met a new friend that was going through a tough time. Her husband worked in finance in the banking industry. Three months prior to making her acquaintance, her husband was released from his job. They were living from the money he was receiving from his severance package. They owned a $500,000 home, he drove a BMW X5, and she drove an Acura SUV. Needless to say, they had a very high standard of living. Within a month after they received last payment from their severance package, they had to make a huge lifestyle adjustment. It was extremely hard to watch because we knew they were going through a very tough time due to the decision they had made when times were good for them. There was not much we could do to help as their world collapsed other than to listen and be a friend. Their neighbors did not even know they were struggling until they put their house up for sale. The outward appearance of someone may not tell the whole story. Do not let your spending overextend your finances.

Calculate Your Cash Flow

How long will you be able to meet your current obligations if you no longer received a paycheck from your employer? Cash flow evaluation is critical for managing any business and should be done when you budget your personal finances to help you live within your current income without increasing your debt. Some of the categories in the cash flow evaluation will be your best estimate.

Monthly Cash Flow Evaluation	
Monthly Revenue:	
Net Monthly Income from Paycheck	
Net Proceeds from Stock Dividends	
Net Monthly Income from Passive Income	
Net Monthly Income from Other Investments	
Total Monthly Revenue	
Monthly Expenses	
Monthly Escrowed Mortgage Payment or Rent	
Monthly Utilities (Electric, Gas, Cable, Phone, etc.)	
Monthly Cell Phone Payment	
Monthly Car Payment(s)	
Monthly Car Insurance	
Monthly Fuel Purchased	
Monthly Toll Road (if applicable)	
Monthly Grocery Allowance	
Monthly Restaurant Allowance	
Monthly Clothing Allowance	
Monthly Entertainment Allowance	
Monthly Membership Commitment	
Youth Activities (if applicable)	
Child Care (if applicable)	
Monthly Donations—Church, Wounded Warrior, or Other Organizations	
Other Monthly Obligations	
Total Monthly Expenses	
Total Monthly Revenue—Total Monthly Expenses = Total Monthly Cash Flow	

Finding the proper balance between the money we need to live, the money we spend on material goods, and the amount we invest can be challenging. There are two different ways we can address our spending habits. We can lower our standard of living in order to live within our income. You can impose a strict budget for your family, or you can increase your income in order to maintain your desired standard of living. Your increase should also allow for a targeted amount that you invest yearly. My wife and I are trying to increase our means in order to maintain our current standard of living and increase the amount of money we can invest monthly. We believe that life is too short to live under a stressful budget in order to find the additional money to invest yearly. That does not mean that we do not have a budget; we do. We choose not to drive fancy cars, throw parties for people that may or may not be friends, and choose not to dress to the T daily, all of which cost money that would come out of our investment fund. Our primary goal for increasing our means is to generate additional money to invest. I hope that one day our investments will provide enough passive income to be financially free so that we do not have to work for a paycheck.

The Cost of Vehicles

Besides the expense of owning a home, the cost associated to own and operate a vehicle is one of our largest liabilities. In the past, my wife and I had always traded in vehicles every two to three years, regardless of the mileage or condition of the vehicle. Now that my wife and I have decided to change our spending habits in order to create excess capital for investing, we have decided to get full use out of our vehicles before trading them. Since we live so far away from our immediate family, we try to keep our family vehicle—for the last several years, a minivan with eighty thousand miles or less. I know that vehicles are made to last much longer, and I can get many more miles out of our primary vehicle. But I do not want to take a chance in being broken down on the side of the road with my family. Owning a practical minivan with low mileage is the standard that I have for our family's primary vehicle.

As far as our second vehicle, I have not always been a very good example. I tried to keep it practical, but it is my vehicle that got a little out of hand. I am more of a spender than my wife. I bought a new F-150 FX4 4X4. Granted I do not need a 4X4 because I primarily drive highway miles within Greater Houston area, but I just wanted a 4X4. After I made the last monthly payment on the truck note, I started to get the itch for a new vehicle. After looking around, I decided I did not want another car payment. I decided to fix up my truck a little bit. Customizing my truck was fun, but it got a little out of hand. I decided to install a six-inch lift, thirty-five-inch rims and tires, a customized front bumper with ridge off-road lights in the front and back, MagnaFlow exhaust, and a Kenwood GPS stereo with an amp pushing a ten-inch subwoofer for my two boys, of course. I used the excuse that I am not buying a new car, but we all knew it was just a way for me to try to justify the amount of money I was taking away from our investment fund. Over the next twenty-four months, I not only spent money on customizing my truck but I had begun replacing parts from everyday wear and tear. My gas mileage went from about 17.5 mpg all the way down to about 10 mpg or less. Before I knew it, I was spending about $600 a month in gas on top of all the repair costs. I loved this truck even though it was costing me an arm and a leg to operate. I am not too proud to say that I am not the best example of someone that has control of their spending, but I recognized that I need to keep it under control. I knew, in order for me to replace my truck with an equivalent newer truck, I would have had to spend

$60,000 to $80,000. That was another way I justified the amount of money that I was spending on my *cool* truck monthly.

On a hot August afternoon, after a long day of work, my truck overheated three times in the Houston rush hour traffic; that was the last straw. That evening, my wife and I drove it to a used car dealership, with radiator fluid boiling out the radiator, and asked them to make an offer. I did not expect a lot because the truck was going on eight years old and it had around 165,000 miles. The truck was worth more than I realized; they made an offer I couldn't refuse. Now it was time for my wife and me to find another vehicle. For the first time, I was able to keep my emotions in check, and I bought a *practical* vehicle. We came across a nice, used sports car that the dealership was having trouble selling. The reason the car dealership was having trouble selling the car was because it was thirteen years old with only 45,000 miles. There were only a couple lenders that would finance this vehicle to only people with very good credit. This narrowed the customer focus, which made the vehicle difficult to sell. This car was an old, high-end sports car with low mileage that looked brand new. I was able to purchase the vehicle for roughly $3,000 under the Kelley Blue Book value. The money that I was saving monthly in fuel paid for the majority of the new car payment. I was able to find a quality vehicle that is fun to drive and is not breaking the bank. If you are like me and you know that you tend to spend too much money, the only suggestion that I have for you is to do what you can to keep your emotions in check when you are shopping for new items. Do not purchase anything on an impulse.

As you know by now, I am just as guilty as anyone with the urge to spend my hard-earned money on material items that are considered liabilities. If we are not able to get a handle of our spending, we will never be able to be financially free. How many people do you know that are approaching retirement that don't feel like they will ever be able to truly retire due to the cost of medical insurance or the lack of Social Security? Periodically, there are reports of athletes or movie stars that earn a substantial amount of money or even people getting lucky enough to win the lottery and, in just a few years, find themselves in financial trouble. The primary reason they are in financial trouble is because they never learned how to control their spending. They do not understand how to make their money work for them.

We live in a consumption society. Unfortunately, we are judged by society by the way we dress, the car we drive, and the homes we live in. We cannot get the full picture of someone's finances by the material items they possess. The majority of us live from paycheck to paycheck even if we are sharp dressers, drive fancy cars, and own nice homes. Many first-generation millionaires know how hard they had to work to obtain their wealth. They know the true value of their money. It is typically the second or third generations that lose the wealth of their parents or grandparents because they did not learn to be financially responsible.

How many parents or grandparents buy their children material possessions just because they are able to or because they want to provide things for their children that they did not have the privilege of owning when they were kids? I completely understand that we all want to spoil our children if we can. I strongly believe I enjoy buying and watching my boys play with the latest toy or gadget more than they do when I buy them material items. But is that what is best for our kids? I do not know the answer to this problem. It is a balancing act, and buying for our children is one piece of the puzzle for getting hold of our finances. I am trying hard to teach my children to have good work ethics, responsibility, understand the value of a dollar, and that there are consequences when they act out.

Value of Entertaining

Crawfish boils and barbecues are common in Louisiana and Texas. My family and I are invited to several crawfish boils, barbecues, fish fries, and backyard get-togethers each year. What value do you put on entertainment? Early in my professional career, I worked for a major oil-field service company. I worked as a technical salesman for three years. When you are in sales, the value of entertaining can be directly linked to the total monthly revenue that you generate for your company as a salesman. If you like to entertain personally by throwing a party or having a crawfish boil for your friends, what value do you place on your get-togethers? Does your entertaining put money in your bank account, or is it a lot of hard work with a cost? If you have ever bought crawfish to boil, you know it is not cheap. Are the *friends* that show up for your party truly friends, or did they show up for a good time?

I am not suggesting that you should never plan on throwing a party. We always plan on throwing a party twice a year where we invite several friends and family for my kids' birthdays. We also roast hotdogs around a fire, grill out, and make homemade banana ice cream for Mother's Day; fry fish for Labor Day; throw a New Year's Eve party; and, finally, have a Super Bowl party every year. These parties typically only consist of immediate family. My wife and I do not put any value in spending tons of money on throwing a party for large groups of people that may or may not be *friends*. We would rather put our money in something that is going to pay us back, such as a solid asset. I do not want to come across as a Scrooge. I agree that throwing a party can be very fun and an excellent networking opportunity. It is always good to evaluate your current spending habits. Is the money that you spend on entertaining really worth it?

Spending on Vacations and Entertainment

Another area besides material possessions that we need to work on when it comes to spending is the amount of money we spend on vacations and entertainment. Have you ever heard someone say, "I am going on vacation because I deserve it"? We all need to relax and get away from the workplace and to spend quality time with our loved ones, but we do not have to spend a good portion of our budget to go on yearly vacations. Take a nice budgeted vacation after obtaining a goal that the family has achieved, but you do not have to take an expensive vacation yearly. Some of the most memorable times that I remember as a child did not involve an extravagant vacation.

Are you ready for retirement? Are your spending habits preventing you from investing the appropriate portion of your yearly income? It is not the amount of money that you invest that is important; it is consistently setting aside a percentage of your income yearly that you should focus on. If you are new to investing, pick a percentage that you are confident that will challenge you but one that you think you can realistically achieve. It does not matter what the percentage is—it can range from 3 percent to 25 percent. The most important key is that you start setting aside a portion of your income for investing. With time, you can increase the percentage you set aside for investing as you make additional income that comes with experience and age.

We all have a different standard of living; therefore, the amount of money that we invest is not as important as setting a budget for investing and sticking to it. It is difficult to find additional money to invest if you do not have a budget or if investing is not in your current budget. Make sure you have an outlined budget to help control your spending habits. We all have to have a little entertainment, but make sure you set a budget for entertainment and do not bust your budget.

Be sure that you include a portion of your budget for investing. As you progress through your career, you will make additional income through raises. Rather than spending the additional earned income from bonuses or raises on material items, be sure to increase the investment portion of your budget as your income increases. Before long, you will see your investment portfolio grow. With a lot of hard work and sacrifice, you may be able to set yourself financially.

Standard of Living

Commitment and sacrifice are needed at times to meet your investments and financial goals. When you are committed to meeting your goal, you are fully engaged to reach your goal. Along our path to become financially free, we will always be faced with choices that can distract us from reaching our goals. At times, the choices can be difficult and not even recognized as distractions. I did not realize the commitment that several self-made millionaires made in order to earn the money they made until I read the book *The Millionaire Next Door*.

Many professionals, such as doctors and lawyers, live extravagantly. Many professionals are too worried about their status in the public rather than being truly financially free. The book *The Millionaire Next Door* made me re-evaluate my view on material possessions.

I am a firm believer that we should all strive to live at the standard of living that each of us desires but not at the cost of going into extreme debt or not at the expense of investing. You must ask yourself: if you were to lose your job or get sick, how would your standard of living change? Could you pay all your bills with no *job*? If not, should you purchase high-priced luxury possessions if you cannot sustain the lifestyle without your *job*? First, I recommend that you find alternative venues to increase the money that you earn. When you do, set a portion of the money that you earn aside for investing, and then you can modestly spend your money on your wants. Spend the remaining on paying down your bad debt.

When I graduated from college, I went to work as a civil engineer for a land surveyor, staking highway construction project in Western Tennessee and Northern Mississippi. For the first two years, my wife and I lived on a very low wage, living from paycheck to paycheck. We both were happy, but I wanted to provide a better life for my family. My dad has always let me make my own decisions and still, today, does not offer his opinion on major decisions. He believes that we all have to make our own choices on the major decisions we all face in life because we all have to live with the choices we make. Two years after obtaining my undergraduate degree, he helped me get my foot in the door with my first real paying job. The only catch was that I had to make the choice to move twelve hours from home. The sacrifice that I refer to is the sacrifice of choosing to take a job away from my family and friends in an effort to earn a higher wage that would enable me to provide a higher standard of living for my family. I am very close to my mom, dad, and sister, but I have to sacrifice the quality of time that my family has been able to spend with them over the last eighteen years. I know many people that are not willing to move away from their family and friends to take a well-paying job. Sometimes, I wonder if I made the best decision for my family by moving them so far away. Time will only tell. I know that both of my boys, my mom, dad, and sister have a very close relationship even though they do not spend the amount of time together that they desire.

Commitment and sacrifice can be defined differently for each one of us. We have to decide what we want for our family and where we want to be upon retirement. Once you decide on the standard of living you want for your family, you must decide what you are willing to commit to and sacrifice to get there. The best of us struggle with being disciplined in our financial journey. We all work for our money, and most of us like to reward ourselves for our hard work. Some of us reward ourselves with lavish vacations, others buy vehicles, others may upgrade their home, and some of us like gadgets. Granted we cannot take the money with us when we pass, therefore, we do not need to hoard money either. If you are like me, you can always find something you would like to buy—either wants or needs. It is difficult balancing your wants, necessities, and your investments. We all have a standard of living that we want to live by. If we want to be financially free and put ourselves in a position to retire, we have to invest a portion of our earnings consistently.

The amount of money that each one of us needs to be *wealthy* is different. How do you define *wealth*? The majority of definitions that I have looked up for *wealth* are too general. Below are a few examples:

"Abundance of valuable material possessions or resources." (Merriam-Webster)

"A great quantity or store of money, valuable possessions, property, or other riches." (Dictionary.com)

"The abundance of valuable resources or material possessions." (Wikipedia)

"General: Tangible or intangible thing that makes a person, family, or group better off." (Businessdictionary.com)

These definitions are very general and vague. The definition of *wealth* for each one of us is the same, but the amount of money needed for each one of us to be considered wealthy is different. The amount of money needed for us to be considered independently wealthy depends on the standard of living each one of us needs to be content with. When someone can live at their desired standard of living without being dependent on others for financial support, a paycheck, or depleting their savings, I consider them to be wealthy. If you have to depend on a paycheck, Social Security payment, or are dependent on others to finance your standard of living, you are not truly wealthy. If you generate ample passive income to sustain the standard of living you desire without depleting your savings, I would consider yourself wealthy. When we retire, we do not know how long we will live; therefore, we should not depend on a savings account or 401(k) retirement account to sustain our standard of living upon retirement.

One factor that influences the money needed to support our standard of living we grow accustomed to living is the region of the country we choose to live in. There is no doubt that New York City, Denver, and California have some of the highest costs of living as compared to a rural Midwest town. There are many variables to consider, such as the type of entertainment you enjoy, the type of vacations you intend on taking, even the type of food that you are accustomed to eating.

We live in the land of opportunity; do not lower your standard of living in order for you to invest. If you lower the standard of living that you have set for yourself, you will not find the excess money to consistently invest. Typically, you will put your immediate wants ahead of your investments. Work on increasing your overall revenue to meet your wants and stay disciplined on your investment targets and goals. Work on building your financial intelligence and investing experience so you can maximize the capital that you invest.

CHAPTER 5

Increasing Your Income

Early in my career, when I worked as a civil engineer, managing highway construction, staking projects in Western Tennessee and Northern Mississippi, I recognized that I was not able to provide the standard of living I desired for my family. Like the majority of young couples, my wife and I were scraping the bottom of the barrel. We were happy just to be together, and we thought we were not doing too badly because we had a roof over our head and food on the table. For entertainment on a Friday night, we went to Walmart to purchase groceries and browse the store. Looking back, I would not change a thing, but I would hate to have to be limited to the income that I made after graduating college, working in the highway construction business.

The two most common methods of increasing an individual's income are climbing the corporate ladder through promotions, which come with experience and age, and understanding the value you create for a company. Make sure you understand the value that you create for your employer and what the market will bear for someone with your experience and knowledge. If you do not think your employer is compensating you at what the market will bear for your experience, then find an employer that does.

After graduating Murray State University in Kentucky in 1995, I have had an opportunity to experience both of these methods of increasing my income. Anytime you do not think you are being adequately compensated for the task that you perform for your employer, you should always check the market to see what the appropriate compensation is for the value that you create.

Even though I enjoyed working in the civil engineering field, within two years after graduating college, I realized that I was not going to be able to provide the standard of living that I wanted to provide for my family. I began looking for a better-paying job and landed a job in the oil industry, working for Halliburton Energy Services. I was able to increase my income by 41 percent immediately. I also entered a field that provided a tremendous amount of opportunity for growth. When I took the job with Halliburton, I only focused on learning as much about the technical aspects of the industry. After working six years with many great people at the field level at Halliburton, I began interviewing for my next adventure on the corporate ladder within Halliburton as a technical advisor.

I interviewed for three different positions within the company—a position in Oklahoma City, one in Dallas-Fort Worth, and finally, the job that I took in Houston, Texas, as a technical advisor and in-house engineer at Devon Energy. I moved to Houston in June of 2003, and in December, Halliburton had lost the service contract to two competitors. I was reassigned to an in-house engineer for Kerr-McGee but continued to call on Devon Energy as well. By the end of 2004, we were able to pick up the pumping services for both Devon Energy and a two-year contract for Kerr-McGee accounts. I continued to work with Kerr-McGee in 2005, and Halliburton placed another in-house engineer in Devon's office. The Devon production and completion had requested that Halliburton assign me to their account for 2005 and 2006.

After working three years as a technical advisor with Halliburton, Devon Energy offered me a job for my technical skills as production and completion engineer for one of their East Texas natural gas fields in 2006. The decision to move from a large service company such as Halliburton to a large independent operating company such as Devon Energy was difficult. I was in a very comfortable role at Halliburton, and I was performing very well; but I knew if, I were to stay with Halliburton, my opportunities would be limited. By making the decision to move to an operating company, I knew I would be able to expand my experience and knowledge, which in return increased my value within the industry.

After five years with Devon Energy, two of my colleagues acquired funding from a private equity investor and started a company. They offered me a position with their startup company to help them with their operations and completions with their company. Again, the decision was not an easy one for me to make another move because I had done very well at Devon. Devon Energy was a stable company, and I was in another comfortable, stable position. There was a lot of uncertainty by going to a startup company, but with uncertainty presented an opportunity for a greater payout. I decided to take a chance and accepted the additional risk of going to a company with no track record for an opportunity to the upside upon any success of the performance of the company.

Each decision I made to move to other companies was good for my career. With each change, I increased my experience and knowledge, and I was fortunate enough to increase my income with each move that I made. The only problem with this method of increasing your income is that you are working for a paycheck in order to sustain the standard of living you have become accustomed to enjoying. The majority of us are dependent on a paycheck. As an employee, you pay a much higher percentage of your hard-earned income in taxes as an employee as opposed to generating your income through passive income, which is taxed at a lower percentage.

In the 2012 presidential election, the difference in the percentage of taxes paid in the 2011 tax return of Barack Obama versus Mitt Romney was made a talking point. The difference between Obama's income versus Romney's income was the way they earned their annual income. Romney was fortunate enough to generate a higher percentage of his yearly income through passive income and investments. Romney paid $1.9 M in taxes, which was 14.1 percent of his annual income. As compared, Obama earned a higher percentage of his income as an employee, which paid $172 K of taxes at 22 percent of his annual income. If you had a choice, wouldn't you rather pay a lower percentage of your annual income to the government? Then you must learn how money works and how to make your money work for you.

In the fast pace, high tech world we live in, we all like to see quick results for the hard work and sacrifices we make. I am a strong believer that there is no program or formula that will aid us in getting rich quick. I am not saying that some investors get lucky by their timing, but generational wealth is built with patience and discipline.

Think Out of the Box to Create Additional Income

Individuals that are able to create an income by working on the Internet have always intrigued me. There is no doubt that it is not easy, but it is possible. My wife went to college to be an elementary school teacher. She obtained her education degree from Murray State University. When we decided to start a family, she stopped teaching to raise our children. The summer before our youngest began kindergarten, she decided that she wanted to go back to work, but she was not sure if she wanted to go back to work in the school system. At the time we were discussing what she wanted to do, Anthony Morrison aired several infomercials about earning money through the Internet. We discussed the pros and cons of working from the house, and we decided to give it a shot. We looked at the investment into Anthony's computer mentoring program as sunk cost and did not look back.

The only problem with my wife earning money on the Internet was that a computer intimidated her. My only concerning factor with my wife working on the Internet was that she lacked basic knowledge about computers. Her only experience with computers was searching for topics on Google or Bing, and she did a little shopping on eBay. But that was about it. I am not recommending that you sign up for Anthony's online mentoring program. Even though my wife learned a tremendous amount about the computer and how the Internet works, it is an expensive program, and unless you find your Internet niche, it is extremely difficult to make money online.

My wife worked about three years without a salary before she was able to find her niche. Initially, she began by learning how to code links for tracking purposes and began to market cost-per-click links online. Cost-per-click marketing is risky and extremely competitive. She decided that she did not want to worry about losing money on cost-per-click ads. She decided to take the knowledge she had learned about the computers and started a blog to pass the time. She started the site blogwithmom.com. She began networking with many different people across the country. About two-and-a-half years after starting her pastime as a blogger, she started a new site, advertisewithbloggers.com, and she finally found her niche online. She was able to pay back her initial investment, and now, she makes about an equivalent of a teacher's salary. She loves what she does, and I have to admit, she is pretty good at it. Find something that you enjoy and a niche in the marketplace and you will be successful.

Do Not Let Fear Be an Obstacle

When I first changed my perception of money, I discussed the things I was learning with many of my friends. My friends are very sharp, but they are not comfortable talking about investing. Many of them leave their investment decisions to their financial planner, which scares me because my friends will not know if they picked a competent financial planner until they are ready to retire. Plus, all financial planners are in the business to make money for themselves by advising you whether or not their advice increases your net worth.

Many people fear investing because they view investing as risky. Investing can be risky if you gamble with your investments and you do not take the time to educate yourself. Investing does not have to be difficult. When you take the time to be informed, the risks of your investment decisions are minimized. I know this sounds easier said than done, but if you are reading this book, you are already taking the time to educate yourself. There are so many investment books to choose from. There is only one question you really need to ask yourself: which books you should select to shape your investments and personal finance habits. Focus on authors that are successful with their investments and personal finance. There are many authors that make their money by writing books and by giving seminars, but when it comes to investing their personal investments, they are not successful. They make their money as an author. I have to admit that I am currently on my journey to become financially free. I still have to work for a paycheck, but I do practice what I write about; and that is the key. Take advice from those that practice what they preach. Do not ever take investment advice or personal finance recommendations from those that do not practice what they discuss.

The first step to overcoming the fear or self-doubt when it comes to investing is to be informed and to educate yourself. Take action on what you learn. There are so many people that take the time to read and educate themselves but cannot overcome the fear or self-doubt about their investment decisions. I have a buddy from college that has been talking to me about my business plan on buying investment properties that create passive income. We have been talking about investment properties for the last few years. Recently, he just took a major and very hard step for all investors to make: he bought his first investment property. He took what he has learned and acted on it. I told him I know it was a very hard decision to make, but what you learned from this transaction will make the second and third transactions so much easier. I know this to be true because it was for me.

I have to admit that all investors have self-doubt. Any investors that say they do not doubt themselves are not being truthful or are simply reckless. I build my confidence in my investment decisions by being informed to lessen my risk. I view any mistake in my journey to be financially free *not* as a failure but as a result that I will learn from. I take results from all my investments to grow my passive income each year. Do not let fear be an obstacle in your investing.

Most of us work very hard for our employers for a paycheck to provide for our family and pay down our debt. If you were to lose your job tomorrow, how long could you pay your bills without defaulting on your debt? When your money works for you, an investor will receive steady income without working for the money. I had a professor in college that summed it up perfectly, "We all want to find a way to make money while we sleep." Ever since taking his entrepreneur class, I have been working hard to increase my passive income. The concept of having your money work for you is a very easy theory to discuss and understand. Having your money work for you can be a difficult theory to implement. This idea is very easy to visualize, but very few investors can overcome self-doubt when implementing a long-term investment strategy.

Overcoming Self-Doubt and the Naysayers

All investors struggle with self-doubt at some point in their investment endeavors. The majority of investors have self-doubt when they first begin investing. The first rule of investing is to do your due diligence, making sure you follow through with the second step by making a transaction. Many people talk about investing or read investment books, such as this one, but do not have the self-confidence to finalize a transaction and make the investment an actual asset. If an investor decides to research any type of investment out of the mainstream of stocks, bonds, or gold, many people may advise against these types of investments due to their lack of knowledge in anything outside the mainstream of investments, which I refer to these negative investors as the *naysayers.*

CHAPTER 6

Leverage, Good and Bad Debt

When someone mentions needing additional leverage, what comes to your mind? Since I work in an oil field, the first thing I can think of is a cheater pipe. This is a tool that is placed on the end of a pipe wrench used to provide additional leverage. The leverage comes in the form of additional force to tighten or loosen bolts or a section of a threaded pipe. For investing, *leverage* is referred to as "investing a small amount of borrowed capital that yields a higher return in relationship to the money needed for the investment."

If you have ever taken a seminar on investing, I am sure that you have heard the catchphrase "other people's money" thrown around like it is easy to obtain. One way we can leverage our capital by using other people's money is obtaining a loan from a bank for an asset.

Leverage

When investing, you want to leverage your money. By leveraging your capital, you can maximize your returns for your long-term investments. This will allow you to grow your investments faster and on a larger scale. My primary concern with leveraging capital is growing too fast. If you are like me, you will stretch your resources to begin your investment portfolio. Although I have an exit plan for all my investments to keep myself from getting in trouble with my finances, I can see how easy it would be to grow too fast once you have a little success with your investment strategy. I caution anyone leveraging their capital not to grow too fast. The last thing you want to experience is an unforeseen problem with your strategy that would cause you to ruin your credit score. Always do your due diligence prior to leveraging your capital. As you obtain more experience in investing, you will be able to increase your leverage. Avoid being reckless with your investments.

I am sure that you know someone that truly believes that all debt is bad. Ideally, we all would like to be completely free of both *good* and *bad* debt. My ultimate goal is to eliminate all my bad debt and maximize my good debt. When we maximize our good debt, we use someone else's money to increase our total capital available for our investments. When we are able to eliminate our bad debt, we can truly become financially free.

Bad Debt Equals Liabilities

Bad debt is debt that we take to obtain material items that qualify as liabilities. Just a few examples of bad debt are car loans, motorcycle loans, boat loans, home loans, furniture loans, computer loans, or any loan that does not create revenue to pay the debt back. See Figure 6.1 below for a simple illustration of bad debt.

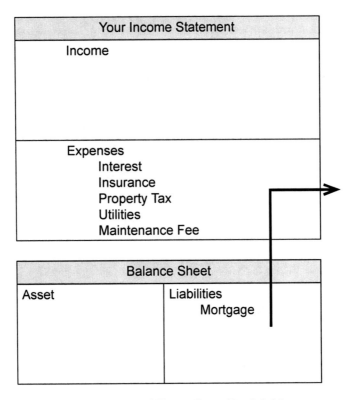

Figure 6.1 Visual illustration of bad debt

Good Debt Equals Assets

Good debt is debt that we take to obtain assets. The good debt is used to purchase assets that generate ample income to pay the debt and all the expenses incurred from owning the asset. One example of an asset that generates income to pay the debt and expenses is rental property. See Figure 6.2 below for a simple illustration of good debt.

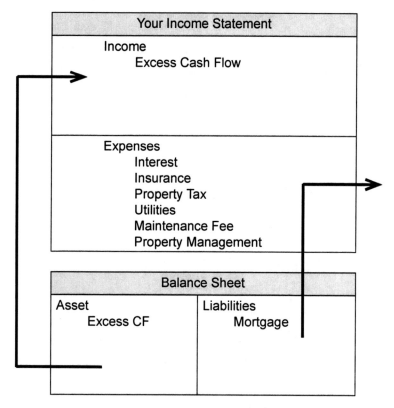

Figure 6.2 Visual illustration of good debt

As investors, we always want to leverage the capital to maximize our purchasing power of the capital we have available. To explain, when the housing market is down and it is a *buyers' market*, I could purchase one home for the same capital needed to mortgage three to four houses with a 25 percent down payment. The positive cash flow from my rental property is very similar whether I purchase one rental property with zero debt versus leveraging my capital to purchase three properties with a 25 percent down payment and a mortgage. The potential that the value of my property will appreciate is three times greater when purchasing three properties from that of purchasing one rental property when the housing market rebounds.

Our journey to become financially free is not easy. Life always gives us reasons not to invest the appropriate amount of our yearly income and/or pay down our bad debt. We can always find excuses to increase our bad debt rather than find reasons not to increase our cash flow with good debt.

Excuses for Increasing Bad Debt

- We work hard and deserve a vacation.
- We had a long day; let's go out to eat.
- We have to have the latest gadgets.
- We like to drive new cars.
- A boat needed for recreation (fishing or skiing).
- Motorcycles and four-wheelers used for recreation.
- Hunting and fishing trips.
- We are going to give our kids things that we always wanted as children.
- Essentially, anything that exceeds our basic needs—this includes extravagant homes.

Reasons for Not Increasing Good Debt

- I think all debt is bad.
- I don't know what qualifies as good debt.
- I don't know how to invest.
- I don't have additional money to invest.
- I will invest next year after taking a vacation this summer.
- I will begin investing when I get my promotion.

- I will begin investing when the kids graduate.
- Any reason you find to avoid beginning today.

Life will always throw us obstacles that prevent us from becoming financially free. We live in the land of opportunity with a wealth of information available for us to learn how to become financially free. You do not have to be smart to become financially free, but you have to be disciplined. You have to be disciplined in your spending habits, your investment habits, and also your relentless pursuit to increase your knowledge in investing and making your money work for you. Our journey in becoming financially free is not easy, you have to be disciplined.

When you make the decision to begin leveraging your investments, the first thought is that it is too risky. You can very easily talk yourself out of making the tough decisions. I can speak from experience; you will definitely come across many naysayers. Many people are very opinionated when it comes to the subject of investing. Many of the naysayers are too afraid to make the tough decisions when it comes to their own investment decisions. Many people take the easy way out by hiring someone else to make the tough investment decisions for them, such as financial planners.

Does your financial planner invest his own money in the same investments they recommend for you? The first thing to ask any financial planner, if you choose to use one, is this: "Do you invest your personal money in the investments you recommend?" If the answer is no, do you really want to trust your investments to them? If they answer yes, ask them how much of their annual income they are currently investing. Depending on their age, the answer can vary. If you have a young financial planner, it would be acceptable for them to begin with a lower percentage of their income. Early in everyone's career, we all should take little steps, but with experience, we should be able to increase the percentage/amount of income we allocate for investing from our annual income.

Many people believe that good investments are risky, but that is not necessarily true. One way to minimize risk is to increase your financial knowledge. By increasing your knowledge on finances and investments, you can help minimize the risks that come with investing. Try to take as much uncertainty out of the investment equation by studying your investment strategy and learning from different sources to increase your overall understanding of the investments that interest you.

Leveraging your capital will help you maximize your return on your investment when your initial capital available for investments is limited. The ability of leveraging your capital will give you the power to control a much larger investment or asset. The decisions on when and what to leverage your capital on will become easier with experience. The hardest transaction to make is your very first transaction. Do not let the naysayers talk you out of good investments. Take the time to increase your financial knowledge and perform the due diligence needed to minimize risk.

Balancing the Ratio between Good and Bad Debt

I can say from experience that balancing the ratio between good and bad debt is a balancing act. I have heard two different opinions about debt: all debt is bad debt and maximize your good debt and eliminate your bad debt. I would have to say, you need to find the appropriate balance between the good and bad debt. Early in the life of my investment ventures, I would say that the ratio between my good and bad was about fifty-fifty. This ratio was very stressful because I had stretched my resources too thin.

The reason I do not simply pay off my bad debt to eliminate all my bad debt is because I am afraid I do not have the discipline to control my spending on liabilities. I do not want to pay off all my bad debt when I may not have the discipline to keep from running my bad debt back up. As I said earlier, we can always find excuses to spend money on the things we want and not necessarily need. Since I know I have trouble controlling my spending, I intentionally try to maximize my good debt rather than to free up my bad debt. I do not believe I have the self-control for material items to truly eliminate my bad debt.

If I only focus on paying down my bad debt, I am afraid I will be pressed to find the additional money for investing because of my spending habits.

When I first started my new investment strategy, purchasing rental property, I had my down payment plus additional capital set back to get the property ready to be rented. I did not have any trouble with cash flow because we found a renter for the property within the first twenty days of listing the house on the market. In between purchasing our first and second property, we continued paying down our bad debt while putting back 20 percent of my bring-home pay for investing. When we had enough capital to purchase the second property, we did not hesitate. Within about twenty-eight days after closing, we found someone that wanted to rent the property. My wife and I were feeling pretty confident in our strategy. The following year, we had put back enough capital to purchase our third rental property. The only difference is that we did not pay down as much of our bad debt and only focused on increasing our good debt. It only took about forty-five days to find a renter for the third property. At this point, we had an additional gross income of $3,300 a month with a positive cash flow of $900 per month.

My wife and I felt very good about our investment strategy. We began only focusing on our good debt, continued to give to the church, and did not pay down as much of our bad debt. Before long, we had enough money put back to pay off the investment property that had the highest interest rate. In the process of focusing on our good debt, we had a couple of unexpected expenses hit two years in a row, and our bad debt started increasing. We had to refocus our priorities and begin paying down our bad debt to get a good balance between the good and bad debt.

In order to make sure that you do not get overextended on your debt obligations, you have to keep an appropriate balance between your good and bad debt ratio. Each one of us has different obligations, expectations, and risk that we are comfortable with; therefore, the ratio between good and bad debt will be different, depending on our situation. I think the right balance between the good and bad debt is more of a gut feeling. I do not want to be comfortable with my debt—good or bad—because if I am comfortable, then I know that I am not maximizing my investments. If I am comfortable, I am probably too focused on my bad debt and material items. I do not want to be in a position to purchase the latest gadget, drive a flashy car, upgrade my house, or go on an extravagant vacation without a little sacrifice. The only time I want to be comfortable is when I can say that I am truly financially free and I do not have to work for a paycheck. On the other hand, I do not want to be so overextended to the point that any negative change in my cash flow forces me to make a drastic change in my standard of living to meet my debt obligations. Life is too short to be stressed about finances and being overextended in debt—regardless if it is good or bad debt. It is a balancing act to maintain the proper ratio between good and bad debt. On one hand, you want to make sure that you are maximizing your capital, but you do not want to be overextended.

Take Care of Your Credit Score

A chapter discussing debt would not be complete without mentioning the importance of maintaining a good credit score. Do not take your credit score for granted. The lenders that can affect your credit score can make mistakes or worse, yet someone can steal your identity. One advantage of managing your credit through a credit report is to monitor your credit. A credit report will help you determine if someone has stolen your identity, which could ruin your credit. It also shows your weaknesses in your credit report, which could help you work on areas in an effort to raise your credit score. The higher your credit score, the lower the interest rate you qualify for when applying for loans to leverage your capital; therefore, it is imperative that you have the best credit score possible to maximize your investments.

CHAPTER 7

The Importance of Setting Goals

Once you set a goal for yourself, are you successful in achieving your goals, or are your goals like a New Year's resolution? If you are like the vast majority of people that set New Year's resolutions, then, like them, it is most likely that you are not committed to meeting this New Year's resolution. When devising a plan to achieve your goals, what are the elements of a plan to help you consistently reach your goals with success?

Elements of a Successful Plan to Meet Your Goals

- Know what you want to achieve
- Set goals that are attainable
- Set goals that are measurable
- Set short-term goals to meet A long-term goal
- Have the commitment and sacrifice to meet your goals
- Have a flexible plan
- Make yourself accountable
- Celebrate your accomplishments

Putting together a plan to achieve your goals is very important in being consistently successful in reaching the goals you set for yourself and your family. One powerful aspect of making a plan is that a plan forces you to think about the actions you need to take in order for you to achieve your goal. Writing down a plan also makes you accountable, as long as you communicate your plan to a like-minded individual. If you do not tell it to a like-minded individual, this person you tell most likely will not be able to hold you accountable because he does not have the same interest or values you hold. The elements listed above are the topics that this chapter will be covering. I hope this chapter helps you achieve your goals. I know writing this series will force me to evaluate my goals and the path I am using to achieve my goals.

Know What You Want to Achieve

Before you can set a goal you have to know what you want to achieve. This sounds simple, right? Setting a real and meaningful goal is not so easy. After graduating college, my goal was to get a good-paying job. I did not have a plan for getting a good-paying job, nor did I have an income target to meet the objective I considered a goal. I knew that after graduating, I was barely scraping by and needed to find a better-paying job. Now, looking back on my goal of getting a better-paying job, it was not a goal; it was a wish.

Once I landed my first decent job by going to work in the North Louisiana and East Texas oil fields, I set a new goal of learning as much as I could about the oil industry. I also wanted to make sure that I built a good reputation within the industry. I worked several long hours early in my career volunteering for additional different projects, knowing that my bring-home pay would not change because I was earning a salary rather than working hourly. The only plan I had to reaching my goal of building a good reputation was through sweat equity. It was not really a goal or a plan.

After working six years in the field, I moved to Houston, Texas, to work as a technical advisor. My goal switched from learning as much as I could to climbing the corporate ladder. This goal would enable me to earn as much as possible so that I could build a retirement nest egg. I did not have a plan, I did not know how I was going to achieve my goal, I did not have a target, and I did not have a timeline.

Each one of these *goals* early in my career really was not a goal but an item that I aspired to achieve. I did not have a clear-cut plan to achieve the things I wanted out of life. To be honest, I did not know where I really wanted to be later in my career. I thought that I would succeed simply by working hard and letting my work speak for itself. I hate to say I believe this is the way that most of us see our future. Looking back, I am extremely blessed to have had the opportunities that came across my blurry and winding path.

Now that I understand what setting a goal really means, I know where I want to be upon retirement. I have a plan, targets or tiers in my plan, and I also have a timeline along the way to reach my goal of becoming financially free upon retirement. I also have flexibility in my plan to allow for me to adjust for life's unexpected curveballs. I have seen several of my uncles, grandparents, and friends forced into early retirement by companies that they had been loyal to for twenty-five to thirty years that forced them into early retirement or into a different job due to the salary and benefits they were earning as they approached the later years in their career. Each one of them was not able to retire on their own timeline; they were forced to retire at their company's whim.

My goal is to become financially free by the age of fifty-five years old. I do not want to have to lower my standard of living upon retirement, and I do not want to be forced into retirement on someone else's timeline. I want to control my future by becoming financially free so I am not working for a paycheck. I want the money I am currently earning working for me when I retire. I understand that this sounds like another wish, just like the ones I described early in my career. The difference is I know where I want to be, I have a plan to achieving financial freedom, I have targets and tiers along the way to measure my progress, and I have a timeline.

Set Goals That Are Attainable

Setting a goal is not necessarily an easy task. All your goals should be attainable, and they need to challenge you as well. If you set goals that you are not capable of attaining, you will most likely get discouraged, and you will not strive or follow through the actions needed to meet your goal. On the other hand, your goal should not be so easy that you are not challenged to push yourself to attain your goals as well.

Early in my career, I would not have had such an ambitious goal as I have today; but early in my career, I did not know how to set a real goal. In about 2007, I began reading and learning a different way of thinking about money, which made me take a serious look at what I was going to achieve with the career path that I was on at the time. I decided to take my planning for retirement in a completely different direction. I learned about setting goals and took a different view on money. I decided that I did not want to have to work for a paycheck to provide for the standard of living that I desire. The more I learn, the more aggressive my goal has become.

When I first set my goal of becoming financially free, I set a goal of earning $150,000 of passive income a year by my fifty-fifth birthday. About two years in my journey to financial freedom, I increased the goal of earning a yearly passive income of $150,000 to $300,000 by the age of fifty-five. I know this goal appears to be very ambitious, but I am determined to meet my goal. As I work toward my goal, the more confident I become that I will reach my overall goal. Over that last couple of months, I have set my overall goal slightly higher. My original goal did not mention the ratio between good and bad debt; therefore, I am determined to pay down all my bad debt and maximize my good debt as my cash flow increases. The key is paying off my bad debt before I make the decision to retire from my *job*.

Initially, I set a goal of purchasing one investment property each year. It did not take long to realize that I was not going to have enough capital available to meet this tier or target of purchasing an investment property each year. I had to adjust my initial target of purchasing one property a year to allocating a percentage of my yearly income to my investment properties. I know that my cash flow will increase with time, and I will be able to increase my frequency of purchases as my cash flow increases; therefore, I am still on track to meet my overall goal of generating $300,000 a year in passive income. I am not going to let the lack of capital early in my journey to financial freedom discourage me from meeting my overall goal. Once I allocate resources to my investments, I do not intend on using any of the cash flow for anything other than growing my investments so that I will meet my ambitious goal of generating $300,000 of passive income by the age of fifty-five.

Set a long-term goal that is attainable. Make sure that your plan for achieving your goal is flexible. Most—if not all—plans for reaching your goal will underestimate some aspect of your journey, and your plan must be flexible. You need to have a timeline, and aspects of your plan must be measurable. If your steps, tiers, or targets along your journey to financial freedom are too aggressive, do not get discouraged; just adjust your plan to the additional knowledge you have learned from implementing your plan.

Set Goals That Are Measurable

What is a goal to you? Is your goal an objective, a vision, a dream, a wish, or a plan? Are you striving to hit your goal successfully? Is your goal to become financially free and drive repeated success? Do you measure your actions to help evaluate whether or not you are working toward reaching your goal? If you are not, how will you know if you are on track to meeting your goals? How will you know if the actions you are taking to reach a goal are helping you reach your overall goal? Did these questions get you thinking about your goals? I hope so because that is why I asked them. Are you confident that you are on the right path for meeting your goal? Hopefully, you have a true goal and not just a dream or a wish. In order for your goals to be reached with repeatable success, you must set goals that are measurable. Below are the aspects that should be measured in any plan for reaching your goal.

Measurable Aspects of a Goal

- You should have a quantity associated with your goal.
- You should set a dollar amount as a target.
- You should set a timeline for both your quantity and dollar amount.

When I set my timeline for my overall goal to become financially free, I set an eighteen-year timeline to own approximately fifteen to eighteen investment properties that generate $150,000 a year in passive income. This may seem to be a dream or a wish when I first set my goal because I had no experience in purchasing investment properties. I hope you are thinking that my goal is measurable but wondering how I am going to know if I am on the proper path to reach a goal eighteen years in the future. Part of my plan for reaching my eighteen-year goal to be financially free so I am not dependent on a paycheck is setting yearly targets or tiers within my plan to measure and evaluate yearly. Each year is one step toward reaching my goal successfully. At the end of each year, I evaluate my progress and priorities and adjust my plan to stay on the right path to reach my goal.

Set Short-Term Goals to Meet a Long-Term Goal

When you set your goals, you have to know what you want for your family and where you want to be in a given amount of time. In 2008, I set my goal to become financially free in eighteen years, generating a minimum of $150,000 in passive income a year with a total of fifteen to eighteen investment properties. This goal is definitely measurable, but the timeline is so far in the future it would be very easy to get distracted from meeting my goal in the given timeline. For this reason, I have set short-term goals to measure yearly to help me meet my long-term goal of being financially free in eighteen years without getting distracted.

Yearly Steps to Reach My Goal

- Each year, I allocate a percentage of my yearly income for investing.
- Each year, I plan to purchase a specific number of investment properties.
- Each year, I set a target for expected monthly cash flow for my investment properties.

I left my steps open ended to allow flexibility to be adjusted each year. At the beginning of each year, I set a specific percentage of my yearly income for investing. I determine how I intend on investing the money I withhold yearly, which enables me to set a specific number of investment properties to invest for the given year. I evaluate my yearly expenses along with my expected gross earnings to estimate my monthly cash flow from my investment properties. For those of you that are not accustomed to setting aside a portion of your yearly income for investing, you should pick a number that you are confident that you can meet. As your take-home income increases with your experience, incrementally increase the percentage that you allocate for investing. It will not take long, assuming you are disciplined and you stick to your plan before you accumulate a nice investment portfolio.

Commitment and Sacrifice to Meet Your Goals

Both commitment and sacrifice are needed at times to meet your investments and financial goals. When you are committed to meeting your goal, you are fully engaged to reach your goal. Along our path to financial freedom, we will always be faced with choices that can distract us from reaching our goals. At times, the choices can be difficult and not even recognized as distractions.

I am a firm believer that we should all strive to live at the standard of living that each of us desires but not at the cost of going into extreme debt or not at the expense of investing. You must ask yourself, if you were to lose your job or got sick, how would your standard of living change? Could you pay all your bills with no *job*? If not, should you purchase high-priced luxury possessions if you cannot sustain the lifestyle without your *job*? First, I recommend that you find alternative venues to increase the money that you earn. When you find these venues, set a portion of the money that you earn aside for investing and then you can modestly spend your money on your wants. Spend the remaining on paying down your bad debt.

When I first graduated from college, I went to work as a civil engineer for a land surveyor, staking highway construction project in Western Tennessee and Northern Mississippi. For the first two years, my wife and I lived on a very low wage, living from paycheck to paycheck. We both were happy, but I wanted to provide a better life for my family. Two years after graduating college, my dad helped me get my foot in the door with my first real paying job. The only catch was that I had to make the choice to move twelve hours from home. The sacrifice that I refer to is the sacrifice of choosing to take a job away from my family in an effort to earn a higher wage, which would enable me to provide more for my family. I know many people that are not willing to move away from their family and friends to take a well-paying job. Sometimes I wonder if I made the best decision for my family by moving them so far away from our family and friends; time will only tell. I know that my boys and my mom, dad, and sister have a very close relationship even though they do not spend the amount of time together that they desire.

Commitment and sacrifice can be defined differently for each one of us. We have to decide what we want for our family and where we want to be upon retirement. Once you know that you have decided what you are willing to commit to and sacrifice to get there, you have to decide what your priorities are and what you are willing to do to meet your aspirations.

Your Plan Should Be Flexible

When you make a plan to meet or make your goals, you have to allow flexibility in your plan to address unexpected occurrences that arise in your path to meet your goal. Regardless of how well of a planner you are or even the amount of experience you have at investing, it is very common for everyone to underestimate one aspect or another in your plan to reaching your investing goals; therefore, you should always have alternatives—otherwise known as a plan B—in your plan. Just as any business plan should have an "exit strategy," you should always allow for flexibility in your plan for meeting your financial goals.

When I first made my plan to earn $150,000 a year with fifteen to eighteen investment properties by the age of fifty-five, I planned to purchase one investment property each year. I underestimated the amount of upfront capital needed to generate ample cash flow to meet the expectation of purchasing one investment property a year. I adjusted my plan from purchasing one investment property each year to allocating a portion or percentage of my take-home income from my *job* each year rather than focusing on the number of investment properties I purchase each year. I still anticipate meeting my overall goal because as my cash flow increases each year, I will accelerate the number of investment properties I purchase. I do my best not to pull any money out of the money I have set aside for investing. A good rule to live by when investing is that once you allocate resources for investing, do not pull money from your investments. I hate to say never, so in your plan, set milestones along your journey with a predetermined value of your investments you plan to reward yourself and your family with. Just remember that you do not want to distract yourself from reaching your overall goal, but it is human nature to receive positive incentives along your path to reach your goal. Enjoy your success along the way to reaching your goal. Incentives can act as a motivator and help you to stay with your investment plan to reach your goal.

Make Yourself Accountable

Most of us are taught as children that failing in a task is a negative aspect in life; therefore, we fear that if we struggle or stub our toe in our pursuit to meeting a goal, others may view us as *failures*. From an early age, we are taught to perform well in school, to perform well in athletics, and to perform well at our *job*. We are pushed not to fail. If we make a mistake or fail, it was and is still today viewed as negative. For this reason, most of us are wary to share our aspirations, expectations, and even goals in life because we do not want to be viewed as a failure if we do not achieve our goals.

Everyone makes mistakes in life; investing is no exception. Anyone that tells you that they have not made a mistake with their investments is not being honest with you or simply do not make their own investment decisions. Making mistakes is part of being human and should not be viewed as a failure. Instead, mistakes should be viewed as learning opportunities. Those that do not learn from their mistakes are destined to fail again. We all are going to make mistakes, but learning from our mistakes and not repeating the same mistake twice is key to reaching your end goal.

Once you set your goal and develop a plan, make sure you tell your friends and your peers that are close to you about your plan and goals. Hopefully, you surround yourself with like-minded individuals that have the similar interests that can help you discuss different strategies. You will be able to learn from one another's experiences, and you might learn something to help you refine your plan to increase the likelihood that you will be able to achieve your goal.

Of course, when you discuss your plan, you will always run across *naysayers*. These types of individuals are afraid to take on risks, and most likely, they do not have experience because they let their fear of failure be an obstacle for investing. Try to surround yourself with individuals with similar goals and aspirations so you can learn from one another's experiences. Make sure you communicate your plan for meeting a goal to make yourself accountable. By making yourself accountable to others, you are more likely to take action on your plan to meet your goal.

Writing this book is a good example of one way that I am making myself accountable for reaching my overall goal. I have shared many of my thoughts and lofty goals. No one has a crystal ball and can tell what the future will hold. Even as I wrote this chapter, I had to ask myself if I really wanted to share my fifteen-year goal. I have told my wife several times that I do not want to look back on our life and say, "If we only would have . . ." That is another reason for writing this book. I did not want to say that I should have shared my experiences in writing. Anytime I have any self-doubt (writing this book included), I typically turn to my wife and say, "We may be flat broke when we retire. I would rather be broke going down swinging rather than being broke because I was too scared to try."

Celebrate Your Accomplishments

The need to reward ourselves is common when we work hard and sacrifice for the money that we earn. One aspect of your plan to meet your goals should incorporate rewards when you hit your targets or tiers in your plan. A common reason for many people stopping their quest to meet a goal is when the perceived sacrifice and effort exceeds the value they expect to receive when they reach their goal. Although each goal you set should stretch your resources, your goal must be one you can achieve with reasonable sacrifice and effort.

The tiers in your plan should have a timeline and net earnings. From the net revenue, you should allocate a percentage of your net earnings for a reward to celebrate your accomplishment. It is very important not to let your reward distract you from achieving your next tier or end goal in the planned timeline. We work hard to enjoy what we earn, but we cannot use our hard work and sacrifice as an excuse not to remain disciplined in our pursuit. Controlling spending is difficult for most of us—especially for me. Although I understand the importance of investing, I have spurts where I want to give my family too much too quick. We have children to spoil, but we cannot let our spending become an obstacle for reaching our investment targets and goals. Celebrate your accomplishments within reason. Yes, we work hard to enjoy what we earn, but we do not want to have to work our entire life—unless you choose to. Your reward should be comparable to your sacrifice and effort. If you do not celebrate your accomplishments along your journey to reach your goal, you may perceive that the effort it takes to get to the end goal exceeds the value of the reward. Good luck in your journey to reach your goal and celebrate your accomplishments along the journey.

CHAPTER 8

Creating Passive Income

Being a disciplined investor is something that I struggle with all the time. Life throws us curveballs that are not in our planned budget. We all have unexpected emergencies that cannot be postponed. How many people have you heard say, "I am taking a well-deserved vacation"? Many times, that phrase is followed with a price tag. We all like toys such as computers, iPads, smartphones, flat screen TVs, nice vehicles, possibly boats, and maybe even a motorcycle. Being a disciplined long-term investor can be hard to implement.

Why do we want our money to work for us? The majority of us must work for a paycheck. Most of us work for money to provide for the day-to-day needs of our family. I know you have heard this: the more money we earn, the more money we spend by consuming material items. This is a major problem with our society. The majority of our society consumes more than their budget allows, hence, so many people in excess credit card debt. We are taught that the harder we work, the more money we can make. Over the last few years, I have learned that this statement is not necessarily true. What we need to learn and teach our children is that we need to work smart to earn our money. We all should learn how money works and how to make our money work for us.

A couple of my favorite phrases about making money work for you are Making Money while You Sleep and Mailbox Money. These catchy phrases are another way of saying the boring term *earning passive income*. Okay, I am not so sure that earning passive income is boring. I get very excited about strategizing ways to increase my passive income. Passive income is income that you generate without physically working for it.

Ways to Generate Passive Income

- Vending businesses
- Online marketing
- Rental property
- Stocks dividends
- Mutual funds
- Royalties from mineral rights
- Royalties from copyrights
- Laundry mats
- Car washes
- Private investing (angel investors)

Above are just a few examples of ways to generate passive income. If it were easy to generate passive income, there would be less people struggling with credit card or personal debt.

There are two major hurdles to overcome when it comes to being financially free. The first hurdle is being disciplined enough to control your finances in order to build excess capital to begin investing. The second hurdle is to put together a successful business plan for investing in assets that create passive income. It is important to educate yourself by increasing your financial intelligence to help you minimize the risk in your investments. You have to be disciplined enough to stick to your business plan. Creating enough wealth to be financially free is a long journey. Only the lucky few get rich quick. We are all tempted from time to time to purchase material items that could prevent us from implementing our business plan. If you were lucky enough to get rich quick, do you have the financial intelligence to remain wealthy?

Persistence in a Long-Term Passive Income Strategy

There are many different vehicles to create passive income. Most—if not all—investment vehicles are slow and long process for the majority of us. Initially, I have found it difficult at times to stay focused on growing my investments, especially when unexpected expenses arise that are not budgeted. It is just my luck; as soon as I think everything is going my way, life throws me a curveball. I am no different than anyone else, and we all go through tough times. My only suggestion is to keep your head up and stay persistent in your pursuit of obtaining your goals.

Choosing an Investment Vehicle to Generate Passive Income

I wish there was one set formula to follow to generate passive income, but there is not. We all have to find a vehicle that best fits our interests. We all have a different tolerance for risk. I have chosen to purchase real estate to generate my passive income. Searching for property that will generate a positive cash flow is something that I enjoy. I perceive purchasing real estate to be less risky than investing in the stock market. I do not suggest that anyone follow my investment strategy, but I want to share my strategy with you as an example of the way I am generating passive income. I hope with success that my strategy changes over time because with success, I should be able to tackle larger projects. I do not plan to ever retire. My long-term goal is to transition from the oil industry into investing full-time in order to make sure the money I earn from passive income remains working and is not sitting idle in a retirement fund or savings account.

Flipping Houses vs. Rental Property

My wife and I are currently purchasing single-family houses to be rented. We both love to watch the television series *Flipping Vegas*. There is no doubt that the stars of the series, Scott and Amie, are successful at flipping houses. They have a very good team in place that enables them to control their costs—from purchasing the properties, to the improvements, followed by selling the properties in a very short period of time. My wife and I have decided that flipping properties is not the route for us to pursue.

When a property is flipped, the revenue generated from the property is categorized as a short-term investment. Short-term investments are taxed at a higher rate than long-term investments. My wife and I are limited on the capital we have available. We want to put all the capital we have available to work for us by turning the properties into a long-term investment rather than paying higher taxes. We turn the properties into rental that generate positive cash flow that is taxed at a lower rate as opposed to a short-term investment that is taxed at a higher rate.

No One Needs an Additional Job

Over the last few years, when talking to friends about purchasing property to be rented, a common concern is the time needed for maintaining the property and dealing with the tenants. Time is precious to everyone, and it seems like there is never enough time in a day. We all have jobs. We also need to spend time with our family and exercise to stay healthy. I have two young boys that have homework and have after-school activities. If you have children, you understand that running kids to their after-school activities on top of completing homework is very time consuming. The key to passive income is not to work to earn the income. I do not need an additional job; therefore, I outsource that maintenance, and I hire a property manager to deal with the tenants. The only tasks that we have to focus on are evaluating properties to purchase and checking our account monthly to make sure that we received payment for the properties that we own.

Outline a Standard to Follow

After my wife and I purchased our first property, we had a couple of people jokingly calling us *slum lords*. Before we decided to venture into purchasing rental property, we both agreed that we would not own a property that we would not live in ourselves. We will not own a property that is not in a safe neighborhood. We focus on purchasing houses that are move-in ready or that can be cleaned up and ready for a tenant within the first thirty days. The first three properties that we purchased had been recently built within the five or six years. All three of these houses were nicer than the first two homes that we purchased as newlyweds. We have agreed that if we cannot maintain a nice property for our tenants, we do not need to be in the rental property business. If at any time a neighborhood declines and does not feel safe, we have both agreed that it's best to sell the property and move to another area. Our primary goal is to offer nice, clean, affordable rental houses for families that do not want to live in apartments but may not qualify for obtaining a home loan to purchase a house of their own.

All the properties we have purchased at this point are one-story properties with three bedrooms and two bathrooms. We primarily purchase one-story properties because there is less maintenance and upkeep on a one story property versus a two-story property (although, if we find a property that yields additional cash flow that justifies the additional expenses of a two-story property, we will consider purchasing the property). Since we are limited on capital, we prefer to purchase move-in ready properties, which help minimize the initial capital needed to purchase a property even though the purchase price of the property will be lower. For example, if we were to purchase a property that required a lot of improvements before we could put the property on the market, we would need enough capital available for at least a 20 percent down payment plus the additional money needed to make the home improvements. When purchasing property that only requires a minimal amount of improvements to put the property on the market, we only need 20 percent down payment and the capital to clean the carpet and to purchase paint for the interior and exterior if needed. We put a fresh coat of paint on the interior of all our properties prior to placing any tenants to ensure that the walls are clean and in good shape for the tenants prior to them moving into the property. We work hard to offer some of the cleanest, nicest rental properties on the market. By maintaining a clean and well-maintained group of properties, we believe it helps to minimize the time that a property is vacant.

When we discussed setting goals, we talked about having a flexible strategy. Our ultimate objective is to create passive income; therefore, we prefer to have our properties rented rather than selling them. We have been lucky enough that we have had low turnover in tenants. When our first tenant decided to move, we had a decision to make: to sell or rent. We decided to put the property on the market for sale or lease, whichever came first. Within the first month, we were able to sell the property for our asking price. We owned the property long enough for the property to qualify as a long-term investment to minimize the taxes on the profits. We were able to turn a nice profit in a relatively short time period. Going forward, after our first tenant moved out of the property, we cleaned the property up and put the property on the market for sale or lease as long as we are able to purchase another property to replace the inventory to accomplish our primary goal of generating passive income.

CHAPTER 9

Building a Team

Building a good team to help you find, purchase, set up, and manage properties is the key to build a group of rental property that generates good, positive cash flow. I firmly believe that you are only as good as the people you surround yourself with. In order to build an effective high-quality team, you cannot be too cheap. Each one of the team members is in the business to make money also. No one will take care of your costs and expenses better than yourself, but you cannot find quality individuals to help you locate and maintain your group of properties if you squeeze them of all their profit as well. Be fair in what you pay for the services that each team member provides, but make sure you build a team that you can trust will not take advantage of you as well.

Mortgage Broker or Banker

There are a variety of options to obtain financing for purchasing investment properties. Using both mortgage broker and banker have advantages that can be used as a part of your real estate team. A mortgage broker acts as a middleman between the lender and the borrower. They do the groundwork for you, working on your behalf by finding the lender that will offer the best interest rates that go along with your credit score. They compare wholesale mortgage rates to the interest rates offered by a large retail bank. Mortgage brokers are typically easier to work with than bankers because they are less rigid. Whether you choose a mortgage broker versus a banker is neither good nor bad; it all depends on the individual that you find for your team.

Real Estate Agent

Finding an experienced real estate agent that knows the region that you are investing in is a must. A good agent can bring you good deals on property when properties hit the market once they know you are a serious buyer. Your real estate agent must understand what you are trying to accomplish with the purchase of your investment properties. They must be willing to be aggressive when negotiating. When looking for my first property, I had a couple of agents tell me that they would not submit the offer as low as I had requested. I moved on to the next agent that was not embarrassed to submit to the initial offer I requested.

Home Inspector

Before purchasing any property, I strongly recommend finding an inspector that has experience as a contractor. The experience level of inspectors vary; make sure that the one you choose for your team is experienced and will provide a very detailed report after inspecting the property. If there are concerns with the property, an experienced inspector can also help to give you a reasonable estimate on the amount of money to correct or repair the problem area.

Appraiser

Any property purchased that requires a mortgage requires an appraisal. A good appraiser will accurately estimate the true value of the property. Find one that will talk to you in order for them to suggest cost-effective ways to increase the value of the property.

An Insurance Broker or Agent

An insurance broker is similar to a mortgage broker in the respect that they work on your behalf, conducting the groundwork to find the best insurance policy that best fits your needs. An insurance agent is someone authorized to work on behalf of the insurance company. An insurance broker has more flexibility to find the policy that best fits your needs. The same is true when choosing an insurance broker versus an agent. Neither is good nor bad—it all depends on the individual that you find for your team.

Locksmith

The very first thing we do after taking possession of a property is to have a locksmith change out all the locks. In addition to changing out the locks, we install peepholes and deadbolts in all exterior doors, including the door that goes to the garage.

Cleaning Crew and Landscaper

We clean the property in two stages. First, we have a carpet cleaner steam clean all the carpet. After the carpets are cleaned, we have our cleaning crew clean every nook and cranny from top to bottom. It is imperative that the property has good curb appeal. The lawn must be neatly trimmed. If the lawn is overgrown with weeds, we have the lawn treated to kill all the weeds. We also clear any shrubbery that is overgrown. When shrubbery is needed, we purchase shrubs that require minimal maintenance.

Home Warranty Policy

When purchasing the property, you will be asked if you want to carry a home warranty policy. My wife and I have decided to carry a home warranty policy on each property that we own. The home warranty policy serves two purposes. The policy acts as insurance that cover appliances, the water heater, the air conditioning unit, plumbing problems, etc. By carrying a home warranty policy, when there is a problem with the property, the property manager knows to call the home warranty to schedule the repairs. If the problem falls under the home warranty, we pay the service charge, and the home warranty picks up the additional costs. If the problem in caused by neglect of the tenant, the tenant pays for the repairs. Many property managers have their own repairmen to handle repairs on the property they manage, but by using a home warranty policy, I know that nothing will be repaired or added that did not come on the original work order.

Property Manager

Finding a property manager is a critical aspect of building your team. They will perform a very critical role in the success of managing your asset. The property manager is visible to the public. They help to keep your property utilized. They can recommend the price to lease or rent your property to make sure that you have your listing at a price point that the market will withstand. They will also run background and credit checks on each candidate. They act as the middleman between you and the tenant. They take the calls for repairs and schedule the maintenance for each request. A property manager ensures that the rent is paid promptly, and if a tenant fails to meet their rent obligation, they serve the eviction notice if needed. The property manager then wires the rent straight to your account. A property manager enables us to turn property into a true passive income stream.

Third Party Walk-Through to Audit Property

In addition to the property manager, we also hire a third party to audit and submit a detailed report with pictures on the property annually. We choose to use an unbiased party to report on how well the property is maintained. The report indicates that there is maintenance required to the property. We have the property manager to schedule the work that is needed. If there is any concern with the way the tenant is maintaining the property, we have the property manager address the concern.

Accountant and Real Estate Attorney

I am neither an accountant nor an attorney; please seek a professional for your advice. I recommend finding an accountant that keeps up with the changes to the complex tax codes to file your taxes. Find an attorney that is acquainted with the laws in the region of your properties you intend in operating. If you have been to any real estate seminars, I am sure you have been advised to place all the properties you acquire under a corporation to help minimize the taxes you pay and to limit your legal liability. Be sure to consult both your accountant and attorney prior to going through the process of setting up a formal company.

Building a team and a process for evaluating property to purchase that yields positive cash flow is important. It may take time to put together the right team. Your team will grow as you grow with experience. Do not hesitate to bid out work to make sure you are getting a fair price for the services that you are getting. Take care of your team. Make working with you a win-win situation for both parties. Make sure that each member on your team sees the value in working with you. We are all human. If they see value in working for someone, they will work hard to make sure your interests are taken care of so you will continue conducting business with them.

CHAPTER 10

Recap

If you made it this far into the book, I hope you were able to take away something to use to help you in your journey to becoming financially free. I am an average Joe who is no different than you. We do not have to have a formal education to unlock the formula for becoming financially free. The primary difference between the top 1 percent of wage earners and the remaining 99 percent is the way they view money and their spending habits. I strive to find ways to increase my means to provide the standard of living that I want to provide for my family. I also do not want to have to lower my standard of living in order to survive during retirement. In order to reach our goal of being financially free, we need to change our mind-set in order to live without working for money.

The advent of the Industrial Revolution generated a demand for a skilled labor force, and employees began planning for retirement. Initially, employees depended on both pension plans and our Social Security benefits from the government to supplement their monthly income during retirement. Over time, employers transitioned their employee retirement benefits from pension plans to 401(k) retirement plans. Both pension plans and Social Security benefits are a third party's promise—either from a former employer or the government—that will supplement the beneficiary's monthly income once the beneficiary retires. One benefit of a 401(k) retirement plan is that we have full access to the money once we retire, but the negative is that it acts as a savings account that is depleted with time.

The alternative to pensions, Social Security benefits, and a 401(k) retirement plan is purchasing assets that create positive cash flow. Assets that create positive cash flow retain their value and can even appreciate with time. Assets can be passed down to younger generations. We must be able to understand what makes an item an asset or a liability. An asset puts money in the bank after the purchase price and expenses are paid. A liability is an item that takes money out of our bank after all the expenses are paid. In order to be truly financially free, we need to focus on maximizing the money we spend on assets rather than liabilities.

In order to maximize the assets we purchase rather than spending our hard-earned money on liabilities, we have to be in control of our spending habits. Spending habits of the top 1 percent of wage earners is the primary difference from that of the remaining 99 percent of wage earners. The top 1 percent of wage earners focuses their spending habits on purchasing items that pay them back rather than cost them money. The top 1 percent of wage earners understands how to make their money work for them.

The top 1 percent of wage earners is not born with the understanding of how to generate passive income, but just because someone obtains a formal education does not automatically mean they understand personal finance either. There are many professionals that earned a formal education from a college or university that struggle with their personal finance. Just because someone is making a lot of money at their job does not mean they will be able to retire without dropping their standard of living when they do. The saying that "the more you make, the more you spend" is very true. There are several professionals—such as doctors and lawyers—that work at maintaining a specific public image that comes with a price tag in order to network with their peers and friends.

A formal education may not be required to become financially free, but you have to take the initiative to learn how to make money work for you. There are a variety of venues to learn about generating passive income—from reading books, reading blogs on the Internet, watching business shows on cable networks, and attending investment seminars. We work hard to earn a paycheck to provide for our family. It is hard to stay motivated to learn how to earn passive income after working ten-, twelve-, or fourteen-hour days, not to count the time needed to keep your children busy in after-school activities and helping them with their homework. We cannot afford to let someone take care of our personal finances for us. We need to take ownership of our finances rather than passing the buck to a third-party financial advisor. We need to work just as hard, learning how to spend our money as we do to earn our money through a paycheck.

Life is too short for us not to enjoy the money we earn. I do not recommend lowering the standard of living we desire to provide for our family. We must search for ways to make additional money for purchasing assets. We cannot let our desire for a specific standard of living exceed the income that we earn. There are ways to increase our income. Most of us increase our income with age and experience. Increasing your income outside climbing the corporate ladder is not an easy task. You may have to think out of the box and do things differently than the majority of the remaining 99 percent of wage earners do. You have to set yourself apart from the crowd. You may be able to increase your income by climbing the corporate ladder, knowing the value you provide the marketplace, and switching jobs to a company that values you more than your current company. You can also find other means to increase your income by offering a needed product or service to the marketplace.

There are different opinions about how much debt you should carry. Some people perceive all debt as negative. Others say that debt that creates positive cash flow is good debt. I believe we need a combination of both good versus bad debt. The top 1 percent of wage earners understands how to maximize their good debt and limit their bad debt. The ratio of good to bad debt may be different for you as you gain experience and increase your asset portfolio. You are the only person that can determine the proper balance between good debt and bad debt.

In order for us to create generational wealth for our children, we have to be able to consistently repeat our successes. We also need to understand where we want to be at some point in the future. The best way to get focused on accomplishing the things we want is by setting goals. The goals we set should be benchmarked along the path of going toward our primary goal of being financially free. Our plan must stay flexible for change when our plan is not on track to achieving our end goals. Life is too short to not enjoy the things that we work so hard to earn. When you reach a benchmark on your journey toward your primary goal, modestly celebrate your accomplishments.

There is no set formula to follow to become financially free. As you learn about creating passive income, you will gravitate to something that strikes your interest. Find a form of passive income that you enjoy evaluating and focus on mastering it. There will be a point when it is time to take your first step by making a transaction. Do not let fear of investment failure be an obstacle. When we learn from our mistakes, there are only results from our decisions; never view them as failures because we do not plan to repeat mistakes. As you grow with your investment experience, you will build a network or team that will help you achieve your goals. Good luck in your investment endeavors.